The B<del>est</del>
Birthday Wishes

The Book of Birthday Wishes

Thoughts and Good Cheer From Groucho Marx,
Marilyn Monroe, Bill Cosby, Dr. Seuss
and More Than 100 Others

Edited by Edward Hoffman, Ph.D.

CITADEL PRESS
Kensington Publishing Corp.
www.kensingtonbooks.com

CITADEL PRESS books are published by

Kensington Publishing Corp.
850 Third Avenue
New York, NY 10022

Copyright © 2001 Edward Hoffman

All Kensington titles, imprints, and distributed lines are available at special quantity discounts for bulk purchases for sales promotions, premiums, fund raising, educational, or institutional use. Special book excerpts or customized printings can also be created to fit specific needs. For details, write or phone the office of the Kensington special sales manager: Kensington Publishing Corp., 850 Third Avenue, New York, NY 10022, attn: Special Sales Department, phone 1-800-221-2647.

Citadel Press and the Citadel logo are trademarks of Kensington Publishing Corp.

First printing May 2001

10 9 8 7 6 5 4 3 2 1

Printed in the United States of America

ISBN 0-8065-2187-2

To Aaron and Jeremy

Contents

CONTENTS

CONTENTS

Preface

As a licensed clinical psychologist for the past seventeen years and the author of three biographies, I've long been fascinated by birthdays and their unique importance in our lives. During childhood, we experience each new birthday as something momentous, drawing us ever closer to the portals of enviable adulthood. The gap from one such event to the next feels almost interminable. In our teenage years, birthdays are more closely tied to specific rites of passage involving greater independence: learning to drive, graduating from high school, and going off to college.

Later, in our twenties for most of us, birthdays acquire new meaning as time resolutely moves with increasing solidity and weight, affecting us in matters ranging from love to health. Whether or not we consciously use a timetable to plan and measure our achievements in family or career-building—something I've never considered worthwhile—we're all aware that society certainly does. For this reason, birthdays often serve as reminders—even "wake-up" calls—spurring us on to decision-making and beneficial change. In this way, as markers of time, birthdays can be catalysts for effective action.

But more typically, I've found, birthdays are psychologically potent because we associate them with our individuality; in no other instance during the year do we receive acknowledgment, affection, endearment, and praise simply for *being*. Think for a moment, and you'll see that it's true. Public holidays are really forms of familial, communal, or religious celebration. Whether watching fireworks over a summer landscape or sharing a turkey dinner with out-of-town relatives, such events generally have meager psychological impact. They may bind us together a bit more, or even heighten tensions among family members, but they possess none of the meaning for our inner selves as a new birthday. Yet, puzzlingly, this phenomenon is hardly ever recognized.

In researching *The Book of Fathers' Wisdom,* my anthology of paternal advice through the ages, I became intrigued by the literary import of birthdays. Especially in today's media-driven culture of "instant celebrity"—when fame and influence are calculated in weeks rather than years or decades—it seemed worthwhile to see how history's famous men and women viewed birthdays in slower, more reflective times. The task has been a most enjoyable one.

In my new adventure of roaming through realms of biographies, memoirs, autobiographies, and collected letters, I've experienced many delights and encountered many surprises. Did you know that prior to the early nineteenth century, birthdays were barely even acknowledged, let alone revered as a special occasion in one's life? For example, you'll find no celebration of birthdays either in the Bible or Shakespeare's canon. It wasn't until the era of England's Queen Victoria—herself quite an ardent birthday booster—that birthday greetings, cards and letters, presents, and parties became part of Western culture. To explain *why* this is so certainly lies beyond this book's scope, but I suspect it has much do with the rapid growth of individual liberty, progress, and material well-being in that transformative period.

In my historical research, I've also been surprised to discover how outwardly tough and cynical figures, such as Mark Twain and Teddy Roosevelt, revealed a secret tenderness in honoring the birthday of a beloved parent, spouse, or child. In other instances, aloof intellectuals like Sigmund Freud and Albert Einstein showed a zesty, humorous side quite at odds with their usual cerebral persona. And still others, sharp-eyed writers like Agatha Christie, Graham Greene, and Erica Jong, have used birthdays as a lens for magnifying feelings of nostalgia as well as for focusing on specific childhood remembrances. Undoubtedly, you'll discover your own favorites among the nearly 125 selections gathered in this anthology.

Above all in completing this wide-ranging literary project, I'm impressed by how birthdays provide a window into our soul's most cherished values and relationships—and as such, a vital means for appreciating life more fully. Thus, we see wise-cracking Groucho Marx humorously congratulating his son, Arthur; plain-talking Harry Truman in the White House coaching his daughter, Margaret, to reach success; songwriter and rock icon Bob Dylan reclusively seeking his roots in Jerusalem as he turns thirty; and, then-struggling novelist Madeleine L'Engle learning on her fortieth birthday that no amount of publishers' rejection letters could cause her to abandon writing as a life-long passion and career.

As perhaps no other event during each passing year, birthdays are capable of triggering deep self-reflection, and eliciting our strongest feelings of affection, gratitude, and purpose. And that, I'm convinced, is what happiness, love, and friendship are all about.

Acknowledgments

This book would scarcely have been possible without the valuable help of many people. The enthusiasm of my agent, Alice Fried Martell, was instrumental in bringing this project to the attention of editor Monica Harris, whose literary judgment and organizational skill are much appreciated. I'll miss her good cheer. I'm also grateful to Donald J. Davidson for deftly guiding the manuscript through to completion. For their wide-ranging conceptual contributions, I'm much indebted to Fannie Cheng, Eric Freedman, Neal Kaunfer, and Paul Palnik. In providing research assistance, Harvey Gitlin and Linda Joyce again have proven efficient. From start to finish, my family was also a source of lively encouragement and unflagging support.

The Book of
Birthday Wishes

Accepting a Marriage Proposal

Clara Wieck and her future husband, Robert Schumann

Clara Wieck was one of the finest concert pianists of her time. She especially promoted the piano music of her husband, Robert Schumann, and their close friend Johannes Brahms. Wieck influenced the compositions of both men by giving them insightful and useful suggestions. She was also a capable composer of songs and piano pieces, though she never intended to be a professional composer.

The sixteen-year-old Wieck met Robert Schumann while he was studying music with her father, Friedrich Wieck. He opposed their involvement due to Clara's young age and Schumann's meager income. Despite such objections, the ardent couple eventually married.

It was during their courtship in August 1837 that Wieck penned these words to Schumann:

> You require a simple "Yes"? Such a small word, but such an important one. But should not a heart so full of unutterable love

as mine utter this little word with all its might? I do so and my innermost soul whispers always to you.

The sorrows of my heart, the many tears, could I depict them to you—oh no! Perhaps fate will ordain that we see each other soon and then—your intention seems risky to me and yet a loving heart does not take much count of dangers. But once again, I say to you "Yes."

Would God make my eighteenth birthday a day of woe? Oh no! That would be too horrible. Besides, I have long felt "it must be," nothing in the world shall persuade me to stray from what I think right and I will show my father that the youngest of hearts can also be steadfast in purpose.

Accepting Time Humorously

❧

Bill Cosby

An icon in the entertainment world today, Bill Cosby is one of America's most successful TV personalities. The Emmy-winning costar of the series *I Spy,* narrator of the cartoon *Fat Albert,* and star of the immensely popular *Cosby Show,* he has also been an active supporter of educational and civic causes. Cosby grew up in an impoverished Philadelphia family but won a football scholarship to Temple University. Cosby returned to college in the 1970s to complete a doctorate in education, which is unusual for a highly paid actor of his stature.

In Cosby's humorous memoir *Time Flies,* the scholarly entertainer reminisced:

> Yes, when I was twenty-one, as Frank Sinatra likes to report, it was a very good year for full court games and quarter miles and 195 pounds of mozzarella-filled muscle. And even a few

years later in that golden decade, when I was twenty-eight, the former Temple three-letter man was still high-jumping six feet five with the body that Michelangelo really had wanted when he'd have to settle for David.

But when I was thirty. . . .

One day after my thirtieth birthday, I was playing basketball with some teenage boys, trying not to be patronizing while I taught them some of my moves. Suddenly, while I was fighting for position under the backboard, one of the boys went up high for the ball. For a moment, I accompanied him and then I returned to the launching pad. A little while later, he also came down and found me pondering a melancholy truth: if a man of thirty years wants to go flying with a boy of sixteen, he had better do it on Pan Am.

What had happened to the temple [of my body]? It was being vandalized, and the vandal was time.

Acquiring Wisdom

—•—•—•—

Ralph Waldo Emerson

Birthdays were important to Ralph Waldo Emerson, who is ranked among America's greatest philosophers. He inspired numerous writers and thinkers including his close friends Henry David Thoreau, Emily Dickinson, Herman Melville, and Henry James. Originally trained as a Unitarian minister, Emerson became immensely successful as an independent writer and lecturer. His key themes included self-reliance and creative individuality. On the day he turned twenty-six in May 1829, Emerson ruefully remarked in his journal, "It's a pity that we should leave with the children all the romance, all that is daintiest in life, and reserve for ourselves as we grow old only the prose."

In *Emerson: The Wisest American,* biographer Phillips Russell recounted this revealing anecdote:

It happened to be Emerson's fifty-ninth birthday, part of

which he spent pottering around the barnyard with his son Edward. Before he returned to the house, he decided to put the calf into its stall. The calf, a big heifer, resisted with that calm obstinacy which has often filled otherwise kindly owners of animals with vindictive red thoughts. The son grasped an ear, the father pushed diligently from behind, and together they tried to propel the animal into the barn.

Emerson hated being heated like this; he often complained that outdoor activities drugged a scholar and unfitted him for his proper tasks. But he was not the man to forsake an undertaking once begun, and again he put his weight behind the animal. The heifer remained firm, rolling the whites of her eyes and breathing through her moist nostrils a milky but stubborn odor.

Emerson paused and gazed upon the animal in bewilderment. The situation was unprecedented. He had read the philosophy of Plato and Plotinus, the science of Newton and Bacon, the poetry of Hafiz and Herbert, the teachings of Buddha and Confucius, the histories of Plutarch and the Sieur de Joinville, the memoirs of Goethe and Napoleon. Only recently he had been through the *Studies of Nature* of Saint-Pierre; but none of them had said anything about an effective and harmonious method of putting a female calf into a barn. Emerson had no physical strength and sometimes lamented that he lacked the commanding presence which awes with an eye, a word. But one merit he possessed in abundance: persistence.

He therefore gave an encouraging signal to Edward, and once more they fell upon the animal. The heifer planted her splay feet and remained as before. The pale face of the sage reddened and perspiring beads gathered upon his high white forehead.

And then an Irish servant girl came by. With an amused glance, she thrust a finger into the animal's mouth, and the calf, seduced by this maternal imitation, at once followed her into the barn.

Edward looked at his father and grinned. But Emerson was already absorbed in thought, his eyes fixed musingly upon the ground. He returned to the house and, after cleansing his hands of their hairy, bovine smell, recorded the incident in his journal, adding this telling declaration:

I like people who can do things.

A. E. Housman

Raised in Victorian England, Alfred Edward Housman is best known for his poetic works including *A Shropshire Lad*. After studying classics and philosophy at Oxford, Housman was appointed to the Chair of Latin at University College, London, and from 1911 until his death in

1936, served as professor of Latin at Cambridge.

Housman's verse was often melancholy, as he decried the sad folly of humankind. Among his most famous poems is "When I Was One-and-Twenty":

When I was one-and-twenty
   I heard a wise man say,
"Give crowns and pounds and guineas
   But not your heart away,
Give pearls away and rubies
   But keep your fancy free,"
But I was one-and-twenty,
   No use to talk to me.

When I was one-and-twenty
   I heard him say again,
"The heart out of the bosom
   Was never given in vain,
'Tis paid with sighs a-plenty
   And sold for endless rue."
And I am two-and-twenty,
   And oh, 'tis true, 'tis true.

Admitting Contentment to a Friend

Sigmund Freud and his friend Wilhelm Fleiss

Sigmund Freud, one of the most influential psychological thinkers in history, experienced strained relations with colleagues throughout his life. He was arrogant toward those who disagreed with his tenet that sexuality is the key factor in human personality. In later years, Freud's philosophical writings were marked by an increasingly bitter, cynical view of human nature. But he had a warm, gentle side.

In May 1901, on his forty-fifth birthday, Freud presented these buoyant words to his friend and colleague Wilhelm Fleiss:

> You may take my birthday as an occasion to wish for yourself the continuation of your energetic mood and the repetition of such invigorating periods in between, and I shall unselfishly support this wish. Your letter lay on the birthday table with other presents that gave me pleasure and were partly connected with

you, though I had asked that the wretched in-between number [of my birthdays] be overlooked. It is too small for a jubilee and much too large for a birthday....

I seem to remember having heard somewhere that only dire need brings out the best in a person. I have therefore pulled myself together as you wished—in fact, even a few weeks before you did—and have made peace with my circumstances. A basket of orchids gives me the illusion of splendor and glowing sunshine, a fragment of a Pompeiian wall with a centaur and faun transports me to my longed-for Italy.

Advising a Niece on What Really Matters

Ita Ford and her niece, Jennifer Sullivan

In July 1980, a young woman named Ita Ford traveled to El Salvador as a Maryknoll College volunteer to serve the poor. At the time, a corrupt government was waging a relentless campaign of violence against students, peasants, community organizers, and activist Catholic clergy. Tragically, she was one of four young American churchwomen found murdered several months later, near the remote village of Santiago Nonualco.

In this letter, Ford shared her most important values with her teenage niece, Jennifer Sullivan, who was safe at home in Brooklyn, New York:

> The odds that this note will arrive for your birthday are poor, but I know that I'm with you in spirit as you celebrate sixteen big ones. I hope it's a special day for you.

I want to say something to you, and I wish I were there to talk to you because sometimes letters don't get across all the meaning and feeling. But, I'll give it a try anyway.

First of all, I love you and care about you and how you are. I'm sure you know that. That holds if you're an angel or a goof-off, genius or a jerk. A lot of that is up to you, and what you decide to do with your life. . . .

What I want to say, some of it isn't too jolly birthday talk, but it's real. . . . This is a terrible time in El Salvador for youth. A lot of idealism and commitment is getting snuffed out here now. The reasons why so many people are being killed are quite complicated, yet there are some clear, simple strands. One is that many people have found a meaning to life, to sacrifice, struggle, and even to death. And whether their life span is sixteen years, sixty or ninety, for them, their life has had a purpose. In many ways, they are fortunate people.

Brooklyn is not passing through the drama of El Salvador, but some things hold true wherever one is, and at whatever age. What I'm saying is: I hope you come to find that which gives your life a deep meaning for you, something worth living for, maybe even worth dying for: something that energizes you, enthuses you, enables you to keep moving ahead. I can't tell you what it might be: that's for you to find, to choose, to love. I can just encourage you to start looking, and support you in the search.

I hope this doesn't sound like some kind of a sermon, because I don't mean it that way. Rather, it's something that you learn here, and I want to share it with you. In fact, it's my birthday present to you.

Affirming Love to One's Husband

Abigail Smith Adams and her husband, John Adams

Abigail Adams has a unique place in American history. An influential patriot during the Revolutionary War, she was married to one president (John Adams) and mother to a second (John Quincy Adams). Born in Weymouth, Massachusetts, to a family of Congregational ministers, Abigail lacked formal education, as did other women of her time. But her curiosity sparked her keen intelligence, and she read widely.

Long separations kept Abigail from her beloved husband, John, while he served as delegate to the Continental Congress, envoy abroad, and officer under the newly crafted Constitution. The two were married for more than fifty years and raised five children.

Two days after her birthday in mid-November 1781, Abigail at age thirty-seven penned these forceful words to far-off John:

I have lived to see the close of the third year of our separation. This is a melancholy anniversary to me, and many tender scenes arise in my mind upon the recollection. I feel unable to sustain even the idea that it will be half the period before we meet again.

Life is too short to have the dearest of its enjoyments curtailed. The social feelings grow callous by disuse and lose the pliancy of affection which sweetens the cup of life as we drink it. The rational pleasures of friendship and society, and the still more refined sensations to which delicate minds only are susceptible like the tender blossom when the rude north blasts assail them, shrink within, collect themselves together, deprived of the all-cheering and beamy influence of the sun. The blossom falls, and the fruit withers and decays. But here the similitude fails, for though lost for the present, the season returns; the tree vegetates anew, and the blossom again puts forth.

But alas with me. Those days which are past are gone forever, and time is hastening on that period when I must fall to rise no more—until mortality shall put on immortality and we shall meet again, pure and disembodied spirits. When three score years and ten circumscribe the life of man, how painful is the idea that of that short space only a few years of social happiness are our allotted portion.

Jane Welsh Carlyle and her husband, Thomas Carlyle

Thomas Carlyle, a Scottish essayist and historian, was once prized as Victorian England's leading social philosopher. His works included *The French Revolution, Oliver Cromwell's Letters and Speeches,* and *Past and Present*—the latter book highlighted the mass suffering caused by poverty at the time. Carlyle's ideas on individual heroism, democracy, and revolution initially had great impact, but his anti-industrial viewpoint contributed to his declining influence by the late nineteenth century.

Carlyle married Jane Welsh in 1826. Beautiful and educated, she came from a much higher Scottish social class. Eventually they set up residence in London, where their long marriage was often marked by a battle of wills. In July 1846, she sent Carlyle this fervent letter:

Oh! my dear Husband, Fortune has played me such a cruel trick this day! But is all right now, and I do not even feel any resentment against Fortune for the suffocating misery of the last two hours. I know always, even when I seem to you most exacting, that whatever happens to me is nothing like so bad as I deserve. But you shall hear all how it was.

Not a line from you on my Birthday, on the fifth day! I did not burst out crying—did not faint—did not do anything absurd, so far as I know, but I walked back again, without speaking a word; and with such a tumult of wretchedness in my heart as you who know me can conceive. . . .

And, just when I was at my wit's end, I heard Julia crying through the house: "Mrs. Carlyle! Mrs. Carlyle! Are you there? Here is a letter for you!" And so there was after all! The postmistress had overlooked it. . . .

I wonder what *love-letter* was ever received with such thankfulness! Oh, my Dear! I am not fit for living in the world with this organization. I am as much broken to pieces by that little accident as I had come through an attack of cholera or typhus fever. I cannot even steady my hand to *write* decently. But I have felt an irresistible need of thanking you, by return of post. . . . Now, I will lie down a while, and try to get some sleep, at least to quieten myself. I will try to believe. . . . that with all my faults and follies, I *am* dearer to you than any earthly creature!

Affirming Love to One's Wife

※

Dwight Eisenhower and his wife, Mamie

Celebrated war hero for liberating Europe from Nazism, and subsequent thirty-fourth president of the United States, Dwight Eisenhower grew up in turn-of-the-century Kansas. He married Mamie Doud in July 1916—a year after graduating from West Point and on the day he received promotion to first lieutenant in the U.S. Army. "Ike," as everyone called him, rose slowly through the ranks during peacetime. In 1933, he became an aide to General Douglas MacArthur, then Army Chief of Staff, and served in the Philippines with him later. Once World War II began, however, Eisenhower quickly distinguished himself as a strategist and leader.

As revealed in Eisenhower's book *Letters to Mamie,* scant weeks before taking the extraordinary appointment of Supreme Commander of the Allied Expeditionary in Europe, he sent this letter from Algiers, in November 1943:

By coincidence, your request for some socks came in just as [my valet] Lee was wrapping up two pairs of supposedly good ones that I had finally gotten out of Italy for your birthday present. It was the best I could do, but if I can get some more I will. Anyway, they come with all my love for your forty-seventh birthday on November 14.

I'm sorry I failed to tell you anything about my birthday party. Lee worked it up and having heard me express a desire to taste lobster again, he procured some on the black market at the highest prices I ever heard of. Luckily, I did not learn the cost until after the dinner, or I would have choked.

Harry Truman and his wife, Bess

Harry Truman and his wife Bess enjoyed a long and happy marriage, spanning the length of his entire political career. As revealed by his book, *Dear Bess,* the former president was traveling on foreign affairs in February 1957, when he sent this letter to her, back home in Independence, Missouri:

Here is a non-forgetter. I am sorry it is not something tangible and worthwhile. It was my intention to obtain something in the

United States Capital of Israel [Truman's euphemism for New York City], but I had no opportunity—particularly after your injunction before I left. Now you are as old as I am, but as young and as beautiful as sixty years ago.

You're the nicest sweetheart a man could have.

John Middleton Murry and his wife, Katherine Mansfield

Katherine Mansfield wrote symbolic short stories about everyday human experiences and feelings. Many of these reflect her affluent childhood in Wellington, New Zealand, and often involve her brother, Leslie, and herself as chief characters. Mansfield's well-received stories were published in collections, in chronological order, entitled *A German Pension, Prelude, Bliss,* and *The Garden Party.* Her posthumous *Journal* offered a fascinating picture of her creative mind and her writing's development.

Mansfield began college in London as a precocious teenager. An unhappy early marriage there was followed by an equally unsuccessful affair and a miscarriage. Her wealthy parents then sent her to Bavaria to convalesce; these experiences helped form the basis of her first book. She later married the essayist John Middleton Murry, and became a member of a literary circle that included Virginia Woolf and D. H. Lawrence. Mansfield was plagued by health problems and died of tuberculosis at the age of thirty-four.

In October 1919, Murry sent this supportive letter to Mansfield, who was recuperating from an illness:

Today I've sent you my little present. Please don't think it absurd. It's just a spoon for you to eat your porridge and soup with. The worst of it is you'll always have to use it. I'm very sorry. But I thought it would look nice on your tray. Will it?

By the way, darling, don't worry if it doesn't arrive at the same time as this letter, though it was posted today and the letter won't be posted until to-morrow. Your registered letters arrived quite a day-and-a-half after the letter saying they were posted at the same time. And I had a letter today from a man in Spain saying that a registered letter took two days longer than an ordinary one. That's worth remembering if ever you are pressed for time with your review. If you are posting on or after Saturday copy to go in the following week, don't register it. Only register if you post before Saturday.

I wonder will this be your birthday letter. It's meant to be. Just for a moment you must imagine I'm under my old hat. You're in your little room. Now I'm coming ever so softly—just tripped over the gold and red plush bookcase—into your room with your spoon in my hands. Now I've put the spoon in your lap. Now I've got you folded tight.

Many happy returns of the day—my little Wig, mouse, darling. This is the last birthday we'll ever be apart—the last, the last, the very last.

Mark Twain and his wife, Livy

Mark Twain, the pen name of Missouri-born Samuel Clemens, is one of America's most fascinating literary figures. In late nineteenth century novels like *The Adventures of Huckleberry Finn, The Prince and the Pauper,* and *A Connecticut Yankee in King Arthur's Court,* Twain combined homespun humor with biting social criticism. But as a father and husband, he was tender-hearted.

In November 1875, Twain, at home in Hartford, Connecticut, penned this sentimental letter to his wife, Livy, on her thirtieth birthday:

Six years have gone by since I made my first great success in life and won you, and thirty years have passed since Providence made preparation for that happy success by sending you into the world.

Every day we live together adds to the security of my confidence that we can never anymore wish to be separated than we can ever imagine a regret that we were ever joined. You are dearer to me today than you were upon the last anniversary of this birthday; you have grown more and more dear from the first of those anniversaries, and I do not doubt that this precious progression will continue on to the end.

Let us look forward to the coming anniversaries, with their age and their grey hair without fear and without depression, trusting and believing that the love we bear each other will be sufficient to make them blessed.

E. B. White and his wife, Katharine

The creator of such enduring children's works as *Charlotte's Web, Stuart Little,* and *The Trumpet of the Swan,* White grew up in New York City during the first decade of the twentieth century. After receiving his degree from Cornell University in 1921, he began his literary career as a newspaper journalist and then worked in advertising.

Publishing his first article for *The New Yorker* in 1925, White eventually became its chief editor in the 1930s, an influential position he occupied for over forty years.

White was renowned as a stylist whose prose works were the hallmark of *The New Yorker's* witty, intelligent, and well-crafted pieces. Relocating with his wife, Katharine, to rural Maine in the mid-1950s, White received many literary honors in later life, including the Presidential Medal of Freedom in 1963, the Laura Ingalls Wilder award bestowed by the American Library Association in 1970 for "a lasting contribution to children's literature," and a special Pulitzer Prize citation in 1978 for the body of his work.

As revealed in *The Letters of E. B. White,* edited by Dorothy Guth, in July 1954 White enclosed this birthday letter with a sizable check to Katharine:

So many times I have felt that I wanted to present you with a fine ruby, or we'll say a perfect sapphire, or a couple of matched pearls that step along together. Yet in the presence of rubies, sapphires, pearls or in almost any jeweled atmosphere whatsoever, I have turned away empty, blinded by the glitter probably. This impotence in my relationship with precious stones has left me a rich man, and you are my precious stone, all the more so because you don't glitter.

So now I have the strong desire to make you a gift in lieu of rubies, and it seemed to me the other night that the thing you wanted was to tear down Earl Firth's abandoned house. So I am giving you that, my love my own. Hit it hard and true!

Aiming High

❧

Endicott Peabody and his pupil Franklin D. Roosevelt

Born into one of America's wealthy, aristocratic nineteenth-century families, Roosevelt began yearly trips with his parents to Europe at the age of three. At home, he studied under governesses and private tutors, and learned to speak and write both French and German. Though never a brilliant student, Roosevelt always valued scholarship and especially new ideas after becoming our nation's thirty-second president during its troubled years spanning the Great Depression and World War II.

Many biographers attribute FDR's attendance at the Groton School, a preparatory academy which he joined at the age of fourteen, as a key formative influence. Its founder and director was Endicott Peabody, an innovative educator descended from the Massachussetts Bay Colony governor John Endicott and the Salem merchant Joseph Peabody.

In *FDR, a Biography,* Ted Morgan recounted:

Largely on the strength of Endicott Peabody's personality, the right people started signing up their sons at birth, and sent them at the age of twelve to a village about thirty-five miles northwest of Boston, in the middle of a landscape that was like the New England character: tidy, uneffusive, a bit grim. . . . At Groton, the boys dressed for supper in white shirt and tie and black pumps. They spoke of Mr. Peabody as the rector. . . . He was ever vigilant for character defects, bad manners, betting, untruthfulness. . . . He made them accept his assumption that the only basis for reward was performance. He made them want to excel . . .

When they left Groton, Peabody stayed in their lives. Often he married them, stuffing his six feet two into a Pullman berth and going off on a round of weddings. Each year, he took the trouble to send each graduate a handwritten birthday card, even though there came to be thousands of graduates. As President of the United States, Roosevelt wrote him on February 10, 1936: "If you had not sent me a birthday card, I should have been really worried! Do you know that I have every one of them that you sent me since after I graduated?"

Amusing a Child

Lewis Carroll and his goddaughter, Gertrude Chataway

The famous English author of *Alice's Adventures in Wonderland* (his real name was Charles Dodgson) was a shy mathematics professor at Oxford and a deacon with strong moralistic sensitivities. His fantasies of magical queens and talking animals appealed tremendously to the Victorian imagination.

In October 1875 at Oxford, Dodgson penned these words to one of his many youthful friends, little Gertrude Chataway:

> I never give birthday presents, but you see I sometimes write a birthday letter: so, as I've just arrived here, I am writing this to wish you many and many happy returns of your birthday tomorrow.
>
> I will drink to your health, if only I can remember, and if you don't mind—but perhaps you object? You see, if I were to sit by

you at breakfast, and to drink your tea, you wouldn't like that, would you? You would say, "Boo! hoo! Here's Mr. Dodgson's drunk all my tea, and I haven't got any left!" So I am very much afraid, next time Sybil looks for you, she'll find you sitting by the sad sea wave and crying, "Boo! hoo! Here's Mr. Dodgson has drunk my health, and I haven't got any left!"

Please give these papers, with my love, to Violet and Dulcie, to gum in at the end of their *Looking-Glass*es, and send one to Alice next time you write her.

Groucho Marx and his son, Arthur

To an adoring public, Groucho was the best known of the madcap Marx Brothers. Fast-talking, cigar-wielding, with suggestively raised eyebrows, rimless spectacles, and heavy black mustache, he had a unique persona in vaudeville, movies, and later on television, for over forty years. In his private life as a father of two, Groucho was also unusual, always employing absurd humor as his basic parenting style.

Upon the occasion of Arthur's birthday in July 1941, Groucho penned this memorable greeting:

Twenty years ago today you stuck your head out into the world, and I hope you're doing the same sixty years from now.

This will give you a total of eighty years, and when you get to be my age, you'll consider that plenty.

Ogden Nash and his daughter Isabel

"Marriage is the alliance of two people, one of whom never remembers birthdays and the other who never forgets," quipped Ogden Nash in one of his many amusing aphorisms. Born in Rye, New York, at the turn of the twentieth century, he started his career in advertising before joining the staff of *The New Yorker* in 1932. Over forty years, Nash published two dozen books of humorous poetry including *The Bad Parents' Garden of Verse*, *I'm a Stranger Here Myself*, and *The Tale of Custard the Dragon*. Nash's Broadway play, *One Touch of Venus,* cowritten by S. J. Perlman and with music by Kurt Weill, was a smashing success. As revealed by *Loving Letters From Ogden Nash,* he frequently offered birthday sentiments to family members.

In September 1947 Nash sent his fourteen-year-old daughter Isabel, away at boarding school, this lighthearted letter:

Happy birthday, many returns and all my love. Mummy and I are sitting in the livingroom wishing you were here with us as the line-ups for the first World Series are coming over the air.

[Our dog] Krag has been whining to get out and whimpering to get in, and now lies in front of the terrace with his paws crossed for the Dodgers. I am still rooting for the Giants . . .

Last night, we went to see Bobby Clark performing in the play *Sweethearts*, and I regret to report that we spent the evening screaming with laughter. A silly operetta, but what a gorgeously ridiculous man. At one point, where all was confusion about who was the princess and who was the milliner and who was whose adopted father, Clark stepped forward and remarked confidentially to the audience, "Never has a thin plot been so complicated."

I hope you are starting to do some writing again. A cable from London says there is a good chance that *Venus* will be produced there by Christmas. Maybe if it makes a million dollars, we should all go see it in the spring vacation. Krag just went out again. I send you herewith a freightcar full of love.

Dr. Seuss

Dr. Seuss ranks among the twentieth century's most beloved children's book authors. He wrote and illustrated forty-seven books that sold more than 100 million copies in eighteen languages. Still widely read, these include *The Cat in the Hat, Green Eggs and Ham,* and *How the Grinch Stole Christmas.* Born as Theodore Geisel in Springfield, Massachussetts, he spent decades in advertising before writing his first book for youngsters, *To Think That I Saw It on Mulberry Street.*

Geisel created the pen name Dr. Seuss in order to retain his real name for more serious work; Seuss was his middle name, and he placed "Dr." before it because his father had always wanted him to be a physician. Winner of a 1984 Pulitzer Prize for his contribution to children's literature, Seuss actively collaborated with his wife, Helen Palmer. Among his many famous verses is this poem:

IF WE DIDN'T HAVE BIRTHDAYS

If we didn't have birthdays, you wouldn't be you.
    If you'd never been born, well then what would you do?
If you'd never been born, well then what would you be?
    You might be a fish! Or a toad in a tree!
You might be a doorknob! Or three baked potatoes!
    You might be a bag full of hard green tomatoes.
Or worse than all that . . . Why you might be a WASN'T.
    A Wasn't has no fun at all. No, he doesn't.
A Wasn't just isn't. He just isn't present.
    But you . . . You ARE YOU! And, now isn't that pleasant.

Apologizing for a Forgotten Birthday

Thomas Wolfe and his mother, Julia

Though he lived only thirty-eight years, Thomas Wolfe achieved fame for his autobiographical novels *Look Homeward, Angel, Of Time and the River,* and the posthumous, *You Can't Go Home Again.* With startling yet tender poetic imagery, Wolfe's writing was often disorganized, but carried great emotional impact.

Wolfe grew up in small-town Asheville, North Carolina, before the First World War. It was not a milieu that favored literary precocity, but his mother, Julia, saw her son's early talent and zealously encouraged it. A woman ahead of her time, she was a successful real estate speculator who raised eight children including Thomas, the youngest.

In February 1933, Wolfe was living in Brooklyn and working on *Of Time and the River* when he sent her this belated but effusive letter:

> I got your card the other day and was glad to hear you are in Washington this week. I am working as hard as I can trying to

finish up another long section of my book, which incidentally I also hope to sell to *Scribner's Magazine,* and my present intention is to work hard up through Friday night or Saturday morning in time for the inauguration. I think I shall be able to do this, but if I am not, I shall certainly get down over the weekend or within a few days thereafter.

I have my back right up against the wall at the present time and have almost no money, so it is up to me now to get the book done, not only for the sake of earning some money, but for the sake of getting back my hope and belief and self-confidence again, without which everything will be lost for me. . . .

I have been working ten, twelve, and fourteen hours a day here for several weeks, and that is the reason I let your birthday go by the other day without writing to you. I must confess to you that I cannot remember the exact date of your own birthday or of any member of the family, or of anyone for that matter, but that simply means that I have no kind of memory for birthdays. I do know that yours falls in between Lincoln's and Washington's birthday, which is more than I remember about anyone else's, and even though your birthday is passed, I want to send you now my warmest congratulations on having lived such a long, active, and interesting life, and on having reached your present age in such fine health, and with all your faculties as keen and as alert as they ever were.

I do not suppose one person in ten thousand can say as much as this, and certainly I do not know of any other person your age who can. I also believe that you will go on for many years longer enjoying good health and with your interest and pleasure in life unimpaired.

Appraising One's Career

～•～•～

H. Rider Haggard

In the late nineteenth century H. Rider Haggard was one of the world's most popular writers. Born in England he emigrated to South Africa and there wrote fifty-eight books of fiction and seven devoted to economic, political, and social history. Haggard's best novels are based on his own African experiences. They include the adventurous *King Solomon's Mines,* published to acclaim when he was only twenty-six, and *She.* Haggard was knighted in 1912. As revealed in the following diary entry of June 1916, his youthful literary success served as a double-edged sword:

> Today is my birthday; a very lonesome birthday amidst all this crowd of strangers in which I take no interest and who take no interest in me—except as a penny peep-show to some of them.
> Today, I have definitely entered upon old age, for at sixty a

man is old, especially when he begins young as I did. . . . My work, for the most part, lies behind me, rather poor stuff too—yet I will say this: I have worked. My talent may be of copper, not of gold: how can I judge of my own abilities? But I have put it to the best use I could. My opportunities have not been many, and for the most part I have made them for myself: the book-writing, the agricultural research business, the public work for the instance. Of course, I might have done more in the last line by going into Parliament. But it's scarcely a place for a self-respecting man who sets store by honesty of purpose and action.

Margaret Mead

Margaret Mead was one of America's most influential anthropologists, and the first outstanding woman in the field. Her most important—and still controversial—books include *Coming of Age in Samoa, Growing Up in New Guinea,* and *Culture and Commitment.* A key popularizer of cross-cultural topics like child-rearing, marriage, and intimacy, Mead wrote prolifically and was named Mother of the Year in 1969 by *Time* magazine. She taught at Columbia University and also served as a curator for the American Museum of Natural History for many decades.

The day before her seventy-fifth birthday in December 1976, Margaret Mead was interviewed by the *New York Times*. She was lively and provocative:

Margaret Mead picked up her walking stick yesterday, went downstairs from her private tower in the American Museum of Natural History, and held court in the Hall of the Peoples of the Pacific: the most visible monument to her fifty years with the museum.

Dr. Mead was seated between an Easter Island statue and a dancer's hooded "fright" mask from New Guinea, which she called "their equivalent of a Santa Claus suit—the boys are told it's just a man underneath, the women and girls aren't and carefully hide the fact that they know anyway."

The former curator of ethnology (emeritus) since 1969 talked about her single most exciting experience as an anthropologist, about a birthday letter from her seven-year-old granddaughter in Iran, and about whether cultural anthropology had any answers to New York City's problems.

"Sooner or later, I'm going to die, but I'm not going to retire," Dr. Mead said cheerfully. "Like a university, a museum doesn't make you move out. I don't have to 'sign in' now, though, and I don't have to observe channels."

A birthday cocktail party for 150 museum guests will be held today, and plans will be announced for a $5 million Margaret Mead Fund for the Advancement of Anthropology. The fund is to be raised within two years, "they can't trust me to stay alive, y'see. . . ."

The creaky-floored, shabbily utilitarian office complex in the museum tower is command post and workshop to Dr. Mead . . . who has four assistants, all from anthropology-related fields. "I'm a tough boss, because I consider them all interns. . . . They're trained to assume that I know absolutely nothing," she said displaying a file card with a detailed schedule of her day, including logistic instructions. "My memory is either not as good as it was, or it's overloaded."

[Dr. Mead also] has a full-time bibliographer, who deals with the complete files and the thousands of books that line the rooms. Yesterday the bibliographer presented to Dr. Mead a birthday copy, the first one off the press, of a 50-year catalogue of Dr. Mead's writings.

"She spent years getting my life in order—now I can look up my own work," Dr. Mead said.

Some of Dr. Mead's writing is done at her upper West Side apartment, where she has a housekeeper, but most is done at the office. She uses an electric typewriter, shunning dictation, but says, "I am not a cranky editee, or whatever the word is for the victim of an editor."

The most "exciting thing" in her career, Dr. Mead said, was returning to Manus in the Admiralty Islands in 1953, after twenty-five years' absence, "to find they'd skipped about ten thousand years—we knew uprooted individuals could change so rapidly, but not a whole society that stayed in one place."

Assessing One's Life to a Friend

Eleanor Roosevelt and her friend Lorena Hickock

Eleanor Roosevelt was respected not merely as the wife of President Franklin D. Roosevelt, but also as a distinguished public figure in her own right. She was probably the most active First Lady in U.S. history, and after the death of her husband served as a delegate to the newly formed United Nations after World War II and as chairperson of its Human Rights Commission.

A role model for women as a lecturer, writer, and social activist, Eleanor had many friends. Among her closest was Lorena Hickock. "Hick" (as Eleanor always called her) started her career as an ambitious reporter for the Minneapolis *Tribune,* came to serve with New York's tabloid *Daily Mirror,* and eventually gained fame as a top journalist for the Associated Press. With Eleanor's encouragement, Hick also took a government position with Franklin D. Roosevelt's New Deal program.

While Eleanor was visiting New York City on her fiftieth birthday in October 1934, she wrote Hick this self-analytic letter:

I wish I had not had to leave you last night, though of course I wanted to come and see Anna. You are a grand person dear, and don't ever think I don't appreciate what you are going through for me. . . . I do love presents and I love you to give them to me, but I can't let go and be natural, and that's all. I will try dear to do better work as long as it matters to you!

You see I care so little at times. Other times I realize if one does anything, one should do it as well as one can, and having failed in Mrs. [Thomas] Edison's conception of a woman's real duty—did you see her interview?—I might at least do these other things to the best of my ability: which, however, is far more mediocre than you can imagine!

Attaining Contentment

Virginia Woolf

Virginia Woolf, novelist, critic, and essayist, pioneered stream of consciousness writing in such acclaimed novels as *Mrs. Dalloway, To the Lighthouse,* and *Jacob's Room.* She was a founding figure of the twentieth century's modernist literary movement. Born into an affluent London family, she became a leading member in what came to be known as the Bloomsbury group of London's early twentieth century cultural avant-garde.

As recorded in *A Moment's Liberty,* edited by Anne Bell, Woolf produced this intriguing diary entry on January 26, 1920:

> The day after my birthday; in fact, I'm thirty-eight. Well, I've no doubt that I'm a great deal happier than I was at twenty-eight, and happier today than I was yesterday, having this after-

noon arrived at some idea of a new form for a new novel [*Jacob's Room*].

Suppose one thing should open out of another, and yet keep form and speed, and enclose everything, everything? For I figure that the approach will be entirely different this time: no scaffolding, scarcely a brick to be seen, all crepuscular, but the heart, the passion, humor, everything as bright as fire in the mist. The theme is a blank one to me. Anyhow, there's no doubt the way lies somewhere in that direction, I must still grope and experiment, but this afternoon I had a gleam of light.

Yesterday being my birthday and a clear, bright day into the bargain showing many green and yellow flushes on the trees, I went to South Kensington and heard Mozart and Beethoven.

Boosting a Friend's Self-Esteem

※※※

J. M. Barrie and his friend Charles Smith

"Nothing is really work unless you would rather be doing something else," proclaimed playwright-novelist James Matthew Barrie, the man who created Peter Pan. This memorable character first appeared in a novel called *The Little White Bird,* published in 1902.

The play *Peter Pan,* or *The Boy Who Would Not Grow Up,* opened in London to immediate acclaim two years later, and brought Barrie enduring fame. He had no children of his own, but because Barrie wanted his work to benefit youngsters as much as possible, he donated his rights to *Peter Pan* to a London children's hospital.

In March 1918, Barrie was fifty-eight. He sent this droll reassurance to his friend Charles Turley Smith. Residing in Cornwall, Smith wrote children's books and was a member of Barrie's Allahakbarrie ("God help us") cricket team:

And so you were fifty lately, and know so little of yourself that you feel "you have lived so long and done so little." I have known many men, and very few indeed who in my opinion have done so well with their half century. You have helped others more than anyone I know, and there are hosts in various classes who bless your name. In fact, you are probably Number 1 of the Smiths.

Boosting a Son's Self-Esteem

J.R.R. Tolkien and his son Michael

Not for fame or wealth did J.R.R. Tolkien write fantasy epics like *The Hobbit* and *The Lord of the Rings* trilogy. Rather, Tolkien wanted to entertain the four children that he and his wife, Mabel, were raising in Oxford, where he taught medieval languages. As orphans, both wanted the kind of close, loving family life they had never personally known.

Tolkien was able to give his children the gifts of his prodigious imagination by inventing fantasy tales for their amusement. When his son John had trouble falling asleep, Tolkien sat on the corner of his bed and conjured up tales about Carrots, a red-haired boy who climbed into a cuckoo clock and had fantastic adventures. During the 1930s, while writing *The Hobbit,* Tolkien avidly solicited the advice of his children about its developing plot and characters.

On the sixteenth birthday of his son Michael, who was at boarding school with his younger son Christopher in October 1937, Tolkien offered these supportive words about a more prosaic topic—namely, varsity sports:

It was nice to have a letter from you. I hope all is going well. I thought your new [apartment] looked as if it would be presentable when furnished. It is good of you to keep a friendly eye on Chris, as far as you can. I expect he will make more of a mess of things to begin with, but he ought soon to find his bearings and be no more trouble to you or himself.

I am sorry and surprised that you are not (yet) on the rugby team. But many a man ends up on it and even with colors who is rejected at first. It was so with me, and for the same reason: too light. But one day I decided to make up for weight by (legitimate) ferocity, and I ended up a house-captain at the end of the season, and got my colors the next. God bless you and keep you.

Buying a Castle for One's Son

•~•~•~•

Sir George Sitwell and his son Francis Osbert Sitwell

No father was ever more magnificently, and amusingly, eccentric than England's aristocratic Sir George Sitwell, and no son has ever made greater literary capital of his father's unpredictabilities than his son, Sir Francis Osbert Sitwell, who wrote satirical poems, stories, essays, and novels, including *Before the Bombardment* and *Miracle on Sinai*. Osbert's sister, Edith Sitwell, was the better-known writer and eccentric critic.

When Osbert turned seventeen, in 1909, Sir George indulged his own extravagant urge under the guise of a gift to the boy—the expense he at the same time condemned:

> You will be interested that I am buying in your name the Castle of Acciaivoli (pronounced Accheeyawly) between Florence and Siena. The Acciaivoli were a reigning family in Greece in

the thirteenth century, and afterwards great Italian nobles. The castle is split up between many poor families, and has an air of forlorn grandeur. It would probably cost 100,000 pounds to build today.

There is a great tower, a picture gallery with frescoed portraits of the owners, from a very early period, and a chapel full of relics of the Saints. There are the remains of a fine old terraced garden, not very large, with two or three statues, a pebblework grotto and rows of flower pots with the family arms upon them. The great salon, now divided into several rooms, opens into an interior court where one can take one's meals in hot weather, and here, over two doorways, are inscriptions giving the history of the house, most of which was rebuilt late in the seventeenth century as a "house of pleasure." The owners brought together there some kind of literary academy of writers and artists. All the rooms in the Castle have names, it seems. . . .

The purchase, apart from the romantic interest, is a good one, as it returns five per cent. The roof is in splendid order and the drains can't be wrong as there aren't any.

I shall have to find the money in your name, and I do hope, my dear Osbert, that you will prove worthy of what I am trying to do for you, and will not pursue that miserable career of extravagance and selfishness which has already once ruined the family.

Buying a Lavish Gift for Oneself

━◦━◦━

Isaac Asimov

The world of science fiction would be greatly impoverished if not for the influence of Isaac Asimov. Emigrating as a child from Russia, Asimov settled with his economically hard-pressed family in Brooklyn, New York. Showing early scientific brilliance, he received graduate training in chemistry after World War II, but soon shifted away from laboratory research to writing science fiction short stories and novels, and a wide span of popular nonfiction books, as a full-time career.

Besides serving as a scientific consultant to the initial *Star Trek* television program, Asimov is best known for such works as *I Robot, Fantastic Voyage, The Naked Sun,* and the prize-winning *Foundation* series of novels.

In his autobiography *In Memory Yet Green,* Asimov warmly reminisced:

On January 2, 1947, I was twenty-seven years old. It was a wonderful birthday, because I couldn't help comparing it with my twenty-sixth, which was spent in the Army. On the other hand, I was more than half as old as my father. I was suddenly aware that I was older by nearly four years than my father had been when I was born.

I was becoming distinctly mature.

I bought myself a birthday present—a slide rule.

I had ordered one from the bookstore a long time before, but there was a postwar backlog of orders to fill and it wasn't until January 10 that mine came through. It was, according to my diary, "A Dietsgen decitrig duplex polyphase log-log slide rule" and it cost me $16. I still own it and it works as well as ever.

Capitalizing Politically on One's Birthday

Mario Cuomo

As New York State's governor for twelve years, Mario Cuomo often referred to his working-class origins with pride and eloquence. His father, Andrea, and mother, Immaculata, were Neopolitan immigrants who came to the United States in the late 1920s.

In his acclaimed memoir *Diaries of Mario M. Cuomo,* chronicling his first successful statewide campaign in 1982, New York's then future-governor recounted:

> Tuesday, June the 15th, was my fiftieth birthday. We had five birthday parties—in Manhattan, Albany, Brooklyn, Westchester, and Queens. The logistics were tough, but we made it—and about $150,000 too. The last party of the night was at the Waterfront Crab House in Queens. It was another of our old-fashioned "wedding-type" affairs. Even coach Joe Austin and some of the

Celtics [Cuomo's sandlot baseball and basketball team] were there, as was [my childhood friend] Don "Cess" Poole—who came all the way from California.

Brooklyn was another "love-in" with the people I spent twenty years working, learning, practicing law among. It's tough to have to ask them all for money and sacrifice over and over. Knowing that a victory could make it all worthwhile for them is a great incentive. . . .

Increasingly, I have a sense of the difference between campaigning and governing. The political structure that is so important, especially in this phase of the campaign, will have little to do with governing, if recent history is any indication. I'd like to find a way to elevate the structure to make it more useful as an instrument for reaching every part of the state.

Celebrating a Successful Career

George Burns and his friend Ann-Margret

For his incredible longevity as well as his unique humor and acting talent, George Burns was one of America's greatest comedians. The wry, cigar-smoking jokester, who played straight man to Gracie Allen for thirty-five years, later found new popularity when winning an Academy Award at age eighty. Lasting more than ninety years, his career spanned turn-of-the-century vaudeville, radio, movies, television, nightclubs, bestselling books, recordings, and video.

As the Supreme Being in the *Oh, God* film series during the 70s and 80s, Burns wore baggy pants, sneakers, and a golf cap. He said he was a bit nervous at first about taking the role, "because I didn't know what kind of make-up He uses." But Burns decided to take the role after reasoning, "Why shouldn't I play God? Anything I do at my age is a miracle." Celebrating his ninety-eighth birthday party in Las

Vegas, Burns quipped, "It's nice to be here. At 98, it's nice to be anywhere." He died only weeks after turning 100.

In *George Burns and the Hundred-Year Dash,* Martin Gottfried recounted:

> Three days before George Burns' ninetieth birthday in January 1986, CBS celebrated it with *A Very Special Special*. Since a birthday, after so many of them, was not that special, Burns treated the program like any other party and sang his heart away. He let the audience take the old songs as silly, but he was enamored of them and the audience could appreciate that as well.

> > Down in the garden, where the red roses grow,
> > Oh, my, I long to go
> > Pluck me a flower,
> > Cuddle me for an hour,
> > Lovie, let me learn that red rose rag . . .

> The special was taped at the Beverly Theatre in Los Angeles, its host the actor John Forsythe, then starring in the popular television series *Dynasty*. Among the guest stars were John Denver, Walter Matthau, Diahann Carroll, and Ann-Margret, who had known Burns well for nearly forty years.

In the past, Ann-Margret had read some of Gracie's lines with him. Now, on his ninetieth birthday television special, he showed her the real thing: film clips of Burns and Allen in their prime. Once again the young and dapper George danced with the young and beautiful Gracie, and the young and dapper Fred Astaire in *A Damsel in Distress*.

Then John Forsythe quoted the most famous of all Burns and Allen lines—the lines, he explained, that they had never uttered at all:

> George: Say good night, Gracie.
> Gracie: Good night, Gracie.

Actually, Gracie had simply answered, "Good night," but a legend nevertheless arose.

Finally, the television special moved to George's closing monologue. The foxy old vaudevillian was now feeling complete; what he did as an entertainer was who he truly was, and he did not have to "lie a lot"—at least, hardly anymore. Speaking about life after Gracie, he quipped: "By the time, I found out I had no talent, I was too big a star to do anything else."

Celebrating One's Father

<hr>

Leonard Bernstein and his father, Samuel

On a wintry Sunday in 1962, Samuel Bernstein celebrated his seventieth birthday at a lavish banquet in Boston. He was honored as a successful businessman with a philanthropic bent—not as composer Leonard Bernstein's father. Eight hundred prominent citizens attended, including the mayor of Boston, the lieutenant governor, and the attorney general of Massachusetts. Leonard Bernstein spoke with great seriousness about the relationship between fathers and sons. At the time, he was grappling with a new composition, his *Kaddish* symphony, in which a narrator, the Speaker, conducts a defiant, somewhat violent debate with God. Bernstein did not complete the symphony until nearly eighteen months later, but its theme was clearly on his mind that celebratory night:

What is a father in the eyes of a child? The child feels: My father is first of all my authority, with power to dispense approval or punishment. He is secondly my protector; thirdly my provider; beyond that, he is healer, comforter, law-giver, because he caused me to exist. . . . And as the child grows up, he retains all his life, in some deep, deep part of him, the stamp of that father-image whenever he thinks of God, of good and evil, of retribution.

This was somber rhetoric for a birthday party, and Bernstein was sensible enough to lighten the mood in his conclusions. He acknowledged that since becoming a father himself nine years before, he had gained a better understanding of the "complex phenomenon that is Samuel J. Bernstein, for he is a great and multifaceted man."

Then, in honor of his father's seventieth birthday, Leonard Bernstein announced that he had composed a new piece. He playfully called it, "Meditation on a Prayerful Theme My Father Sang in the Shower Thirty Years Ago." He later incorporated it into his *Kaddish* symphony.

Celebrating Romantic Love

❦

Elizabeth Barrett Browning and her future husband,
Robert Browning

Elizabeth Barrett Browning was one of Victorian England's most famous poets, with works including the romantically passionate *Sonnets from the Portuguese*. During her lifetime, she came to be more admired for her literary talent than was her husband, the poet Robert Browning.

Educated at home in classic Greek, Latin, and several modern languages, Elizabeth Barrett showed early genius, and at the age of thirteen published a long poem with her father's financial assistance. At the age of fifteen, she almost died from spinal injuries suffered in a fall, and remained a semi-invalid throughout her life. When nearly forty and well known in her own right, she met the poet Robert Browning in 1845, and the two married the following year. They eventually moved to Pisa and then Florence, Italy, where Elizabeth spent her final, widowed years writing poetry on social and political issues including the scourge of American slavery.

For Robert's thirty-fourth birthday in May 1846, Elizabeth penned these words to her future husband:

> Beloved, my thoughts go to you this morning, loving and blessing you! May God bless you for both His worlds, not for this alone. For me, if I can ever do or be anything to you, it will be my utter-most blessing of all I ever knew, or could know. A year ago, I thought with a kind of mournful exultation, that I was pure of wishes. Now, they recoil back to me in a springtide: flowing back, wave upon wave, until I should lose breath to speak them! May God bless you, very dear! dearest.

Christina Rossetti

Christina Rossetti was an important late nineteenth century poet and a leader of the English pre-Raphaelite movement, which exalted mystical symbolism and art. Like her London-based brother, Dante Gabriel, who was a famous poet and painter, Christina combined a melancholy and self-critical outlook with a lively sense of humor and a perceptive eye. For several years, she was the only woman member of the pre-Raphaelite Brotherhood, which she formed with her two brothers and five of their artistic friends. Christina modeled for paintings and became friendly with such Victorian luminaries as Robert Browning, John Ruskin, and Lewis Carroll.

Goblin Market is one of Rossetti's most respected works, a fantasy-poem about a girl's love for her sister. It was published in 1862. Her other major writings include a nursery rhyme collection called *A Sing-Song,* and two volumes of religious prose, *Annus Domini* and *Seek and Find.*

Christina Rossetti composed this beautiful poem when she turned twenty-one, in 1857:

A BIRTHDAY

My heart is like a singing bird
   Whose nest is in a watered shoot:
My heart is like an apple tree
   Whose boughs are bent with thickset fruit;
My heart is like a rainbow shell
   That paddles in a halcyon sea;
My heart is gladder than all these
   Because my love is come to me.

Raise me a dais of silk and down;
    Hang it with fair and purple dyes;
Carve it in doves and pomegranates,
    And peacocks with a hundred eyes;
Work it in gold and silver grapes,
    In leaves and silver fleurs-de-lys;
Because the birthday of my life
    Is come, my love is come to me.

Chastising a Forgetful Friend

Gerard Manley Hopkins

Born in mid-nineteenth century London, Hopkins achieved lasting fame as a poet only after his death; a posthumous collection of his poems, produced by a friend, Robert Bridges, and published in 1918, established Hopkins's reputation. He once remarked, "As air, melody is what strikes me most of all in music and design in painting: so design, pattern, or what I am in the habit of calling *inscape* is what I above all aim at in poetry."

As a young man studying at Oxford, Hopkins became interested in Catholicism and was later ordained as a Jesuit priest in North Wales. In Hopkins's final years, he served as a respected professor of Greek at the University of Ireland in Dublin. Among his poems was this birthday theme:

A COMPLAINT

I thought that you would have written: my birthday came and
    went,
And with the last post over I knew no letter was sent.
And if you write at last, it never can be the same:
What would be a birthday letter that after the birthday came?

I know that you will tell me—neglectful that you were not.
But is not that my grievance—you promised and you forgot?
It's the day that makes the charm; no after-words could
    succeed
Though they took till the seventeenth of next October to read.

Think this, my birthday falls in saddening time of year;
Only the dahlias blow, and all is Autumn here.
Hampstead was never bright; and whatever Miss Cully's
    charms
It is hardly a proper treat for a birthday to rest in her arms.
Our sex should be born in April perhaps or the lily-time;
But the lily is past, as I say, and the rose is not in its prime:
What I did ask then was a circle of rose-red sealing-wax
And a few leaves not lily-white but charactered over with
    blacks.

But late is better than never: you see you have managed so,
You have made me quote almost the dismalest proverb I know:
For a letter comes at last: shall I say before Christmas is come?
And I must take your amends, cry Pardon, and then be dumb.

Cheering Up a Friend

Rupert Brooke and his friend Hugh Russell-Smith

Rupert Brooke was a leading young English poet in the early 1900s, a member of the Georgian group, who wrote traditional romantic verse about nature and love. Born in Rugby, near Coventry, he traveled to North America, Europe, and the South Pacific from 1913 to 1914. When World War I broke out, Brooke enlisted and wrote a series of patriotic poems entitled *1914*, his best-known work. He tragically died in battle the following year.

In September 1905, Brooke was eighteen years old and attending school at Rugby when he inscribed this jovial letter to his classmate Hugh Russell-Smith:

> So you happened twentily on the Sabbath. Did it hurt much? Or did you take gas for it, as I did? With advancing years, I find one's thoughts turn increasingly toward the Hereafter and the

Serious Things of Life. In this small pamphlet from which I have quoted often, you will find many helpful thoughts: notably in the merry verses that recommend the habits of Drinking, Chronic Lugubriousness, and Suicide. From 8 to 10 P.M., I read Roman History. But you are in black woods.

Childhood Nostalgia

Agatha Christie

Agatha Christie, born in Devon, England, in 1890, was acclaimed as one of the greatest mystery writers of our age. She was educated at home by her mother. While serving as a volunteer nurse during World War I, she began actively writing and published her first novel soon after. With the appearance of *The Murder of Roger Ackroyd* in 1926, Agatha gained major recognition. There followed seventy-five successful novels, twenty-five of them featuring the detective Hercule Poirot. *Witness for the Prosecution, Death on the Nile,* and *Murder on the Orient Express* were all adapted for film.

In Christie's memoir, *An Autobiography,* she warmly recalled this happy childhood experience:

> It is difficult to know what one's first memory is. I remember distinctly my third birthday. The sense of my own importance

surges up in me. We are having tea in the garden—in the part of the garden where, later, a hammock swings between two trees.

There is a tea table and it is covered with cakes, with my birthday cake, all sugar icing and with candles in the middle of it. Three candles. And then the exciting occurrence—a tiny red spider, so small that I can hardly see it, runs across the white cloth. And my mother says: "It's a *lucky* spider. Agatha, a lucky spider for your birthday."

And then the memory fades, except for a fragmentary reminiscence of an interminable argument sustained by my brother as to how many eclairs he shall be allowed to eat.

The lovely, safe, yet exciting world of childhood.

Graham Greene

Graham Greene authored such popular novels as *The Third Man*, *The Power and the Glory*, and *Our Man in Havana*, all of which were adapted for the cinema. Over a sixty year career that brought him considerable financial success, Greene associated with many famous writers of his time, including Noel Coward, T. S. Eliot, Ian Fleming, Herbert Read, and Evelyn Waugh. Born in rural England, in 1904, as the fourth of six children, Graham was a shy and sensitive youth.

In Greene's memoir, *A Sort of Life,* he offered this droll recollection of childhood:

I hated the very idea of children's birthday parties. They were a threat that one day I might have to put to practical use my dancing lessons, of which I can only remember the black shiny shoes with the snappy elastic and the walk down King's Road, between the red brick villas on winter evenings, holding someone's hand for fear of slipping.

The only children's party I can actually remember was up near Berkhamsted Commons in a big, strange house, where I never went again: a Chinese servant asked if I wanted "to make water" and I did not understand her, so that always afterwards I thought of it as a Chinese expression. Many years later, I wrote a short story about a children's party, and another about dancing lessons, and perhaps there are memories concealed in them too.

Complaining About Midlife

Dave Barry

Dave Barry, a syndicated columnist for the *Miami Herald,* is widely known for such humorous books as *Dave Barry Slept Here, Claw Your Way to the Top*, and *Dave Barry's Guide to Marriage and/or Sex.* Raised in a New York City suburb, he decided on a journalism career, and first gained wide popularity in the early 1980s for his satirical articles on contemporary family life and other topics.

In the introduction to *Dave Barry Turns Fifty,* the humorist comments:

> I am not going to whine.
>
> Yes, I have turned fifty.
>
> Yes, this is an age that I used to consider old. Not middle-aged, like Dick Van Dyke and Mary Tyler Moore in *The Dick Van Dyke Show,* but actually *old,* like Walter Brennan as Gran-

pappy Amos in *The Real McCoys,* gimping around cluelessly in a pair of bib overalls and saying things like, "Con-SARN-it!"

But I do not choose to dwell on the negative. I choose to be an optimist, like the great explorer Christopher Columbus, who had a dream that he could sail a ship all the way across the Atlantic Ocean.... And so Columbus boldly set out and discovered the New World and then he went back to Europe, where he died in obscurity at age 55, which is *only five years older than I am right now!* OH GOD! MY LIFE IS OVER!!!

[When you turn fifty], you find that with your reading glasses on you behave differently. You become crotchety and easily irritated by little things, such as when the supermarket runs out of your preferred brand . . . of "breakfast links" made from tofu and compressed cardboard. You become angry at the radio because it keeps playing songs you hate, which is a LOT of songs, because you basically hate every song written since the Beatles broke up, and you're sick of the Beatles, too, because you've heard every one of their songs 900 million times on "oldies" radio, which is all you've listened to for over twenty years. You feel that everybody except you drives too fast. You think of people under the age of thirty as "whippersnappers," and you get the urge to peer over your reading glasses at them and tell them how tough things were during the Great Depression even though you personally were born in 1947. Sometimes you are tempted to say, "Con-SARN it ..."

Yes, there are some real benefits to turning fifty. And that's going to be the theme of this book. It's going to be a celebration of the aging process. I'm not talking about just my aging process, but that of the whole massive Baby Boom Generation—the millions and millions of us who were born in the postwar era and went on to set a standard for whiny self-absorption that will probably never be equaled.

Confiding a Spiritual Awakening
to a Friend

◄~◄~◄~•

Kahlil Gibran and his friend Mary Haskell

Kahlil Gibran is celebrated for writing *The Prophet* and other books of mystical philosophy. Born into a Christian Lebanese family, Gibran emigrated to Boston as a child with his mother. As a teenager, he studied Arabic literature in Beirut, and art in Paris with Auguste Rodin, before returning to the United States in 1899 to launch an artistic career. From an early age, Gibran had transcendental experiences that provided the basis for his painting and writing. He met his beloved friend and benefactor, headmistress Mary Haskell, while living in Boston, but Gibran spent most of his creative life in New York City's bohemian Greenwich Village.

Already established in his studio there in January 1912, Gibran sent Mary Haskell this news upon turning twenty-nine:

Tuesday was much more of a birthday than today. The reality of those few hours is a door which leads to a new sense of joy and a new sense of pain and a new vision of Life. I have tried many times since that evening to write to you, but each time, I found myself so completely overwhelmed by a strange silence—the silence of deep seas and undiscovered regions—the silence of unknown gods.

And even now as I write, I feel that the most terrible element in Life is a dumb element. The hours that pass before a mighty storm and the days that come after a great joy or a great sorrow are alike, dumb and deep and full of outspread wings and motionless flames.

Conveying Brotherly Love

※※※

Lewis Carroll and his sister Mary Dodgson

Lewis Carroll was a shy mathematics professor at Oxford who became famous for writing such imaginative works as *Alice in Wonderland*. Academically ambitious, Dodgson grew up in a middle-class home with seven sisters. As a new student at Oxford in March 1851, he offered these sentiments to his younger sister Mary:

> I write this for you to get on Saturday, as I suppose you will not get the letters on Sunday. I hope you will "keep" it very happily on Monday, and will imagine my presence when the health is drunk. The other day, I borrowed a book called *Coxe's Christian Ballads*, thinking I might like to get a copy. However, I found so many things in it I did not like, and so few I did, that I decided on not buying the book. But as some of the ballads are

sold separately, I got the two I liked best, which I enclose. One needs sewing.

I think you will like them, but I can hardly ask you to consider so small a purchase as a birthday present.

Conveying Love to One's Daughter-in-Law

***

Sara Roosevelt and her daughter-in-law, Eleanor Roosevelt

Eleanor Roosevelt, highlighted earlier in this book, experienced a difficult childhood, marked by the untimely deaths of both parents. Self-conscious and awkward in comparison to many of her aristocratic peers, Eleanor met her second cousin Franklin Roosevelt at a high-society bash for his twenty-first birthday. The two fell quickly in love, and were married two years later.

In *A First-Class Temperament: The Emergence of Franklin Roosevelt* Geoffrey Ward records this greeting to Eleanor, in October 1905, upon her twenty-first birthday, from Franklin's mother, Sara:

> I am thinking much of you, and wishing you every happiness for the coming year and many years to follow. I pray that my precious Franklin may make you very happy and thank him for giving me such a dear, loving daughter. I thank *you* also darling

for being what you are to me already. This is straight from my heart.

I felt you were not at all well yesterday, and hope today is a better day. You looked so white and tired.... With dear love and 21 kisses and one more to "grow on."

Franklin mother didn't know it, but Eleanor was "so white and tired" because she was pregnant. The baby, the newlyweds' first, was born in early May and named Anna Eleanor, after her mother.

Conveying Sisterly Love

Victoria, Queen of Great Britain, and her brother-in-law Wilhelm, King of Prussia

Born in 1819, Victoria became an icon and a symbol of her time. She occupied the British throne for sixty-two years, England's longest-reigning monarch. Her reign was characterized by vast scientific, industrial, educational, and social progress, and the ascension of the British Empire to world dominance, with London as its epicenter.

After the death of her beloved husband, Prince Albert in 1862 at the age of forty-one, Victoria suffered from bouts of depression and withdrawal which continued for much of her subsequent life. But she remained actively involved with her nine children and numerous grandchildren.

Birthdays were always important to the Queen, and during her reign the custom of sending birthday greetings, letters, and presents—

together with making birthday parties—gained unprecedented popularity in English-speaking countries around the world. In March 1887, Victoria sent this letter to her daughter Victoria Adelaide's powerful father-in-law:

I cannot allow my son to leave without giving him these lines to bring you my wishes for your happiness and prosperity on the occasion of your ninetieth birthday. Such an age is seldom attained; may God bless and protect you still. It is strange that in the year in which you celebrate your ninetieth birthday, I shall reach the fiftieth anniversary of my accession. And in this year, so important for both of us, our grandchildren have become betrothed.

I cannot think unmoved of the union of the children of my two dear daughters. Henry should consider himself fortunate to win such a wife as my beloved Irene. You were always so kind, dear brother, to my never-to-be-forgotten Alice that I cannot doubt that you will be glad to welcome her daughter as your future granddaughter. She is a most charming girl.

Declaring Gratitude to One's Friends

Martin Buber

Martin Buber, considered one of the most important philosophers and religious thinkers of our time, was the author of such works as *I and Thou* and *Tales of the Hasidim*. Buber was born in late nineteenth century Vienna, and drew close to his ancestral Judaism at an early age. Teaching at the University of Frankfurt for many decades, he sought to recast Jewish teachings for the modern world. His emphasis was on dialogue and deep mutual understanding as a pathway to the divine.

In 1938, shortly before Hitler launched World War II, Buber emigrated to the Holy Land. There, as a professor of philosophy at the new Hebrew University in Jerusalem, he exerted an international influence on psychology, psychiatry, and theology.

Upon turning eighty in February 1958, Buber wrote this *Expression of Thanks* to his worldwide friends and admirers:

The older one becomes, so much more grows in one the inclination to thank.

Before all to what is above. Now, indeed, so strongly as could never have been possible before, life is felt as an unearned gift, and especially each hour that is entirely good one, one receives, like a surprising present, with outstretched thankful hands.

But after that, it is necessary time and again to thank one's fellow man, even when he has not done anything especially for one. For what, then? For the fact that when he met me, he had really met me, that he opened his eyes and did not confuse me with anyone else, that he opened his ears and reliably heard what I had to say to him: yes, that he opened what I really addressed, his well-closed heart.

The hour in which I write is an hour of great thanks; before me is a beautiful giant box set here by my granddaughter and containing all the congratulations received on this milestone day of my life-way from those who on the way have met me bodily or spiritually, *and in my memory,* are all the direct congratulations.

The thanks I say here to all are not directed to a totality, but to each individual.

Declaring Gratitude to One's Son

Margaret Ogilvy Barrie and her son J. M. Barrie

Margaret Ogilvy Barrie is best known today as the mother of playwright-novelist James Matthew Barrie, creator of Peter Pan. She was married to a weaver, David Barrie, and raised nine children in mid-nineteenth-century rural Scotland. In 1892, Margaret Barrie sent this letter to James, who, together with his wife, Mary, was caring for his sister, Maggie, after the death of her fiancé. At the time, Barrie had just seen the publication of his first novel, *The Little Minister.*

My heart keeps blessing and thanking you, but no words can say my love. My heart fails in words for my first birthday gift.

My dear beloved son, God bless you and prosper you. You are a precious, God-given son to me, the light of my eyes—and my darling Maggie is safe with God and you till we meet.

Describing a Big Bash to a Friend

❦

Walt Whitman and his friend Dr. Richard Bucke

Walt Whitman is considered one of America's greatest poets, best known for his collection of verse *Leaves of Grass*. Born into a poor family on Long Island, New York, he was raised in Brooklyn and quit school at the age of twelve to become a printer's assistant. Whitman worked as a schoolteacher, printer, and journalist in the New York City area, and became known for his incisive articles on political issues, civic affairs, and the arts.

During the Civil War, Whitman was a government clerk and a volunteer assistant in the military hospital of Washington, D.C. After the war, he served in several governmental departments until a stroke in 1873 restricted his activities. Retiring to Camden, New Jersey, Whitman continued for nearly twenty years to write poems and articles.

In June 1889, he sent his longtime friend—the Canadian physician and mystical philosopher Richard Bucke—this letter:

Well, here I am, feeling fairly, commencing my 71st year. The dinner last evening came off and went off all right, and was a great success. They say it was a mighty good *dinner* (nothing to drink but Apollinaris water) I was not at the eating part, but went an hour later. Ed wheeled me in the chair, and two policemen and two other good fellows carried me from the sidewalk, chair and all as I sat, up the stairs and turning (which were fortunately wide and easy) to the big banquet hall and big crowd.

I was rolled to my seat, and after being received with tremendous cheering, they brought me a bottle of first-rate champagne and a big glass with ice. The whole thing was tip-top, and luckily I felt better and more something like myself, and nearer chipper, than for a year. The compliments and eulogies to me were excessive and without break. But I filled my ice-glass with the good wine, and picked out two fragrant roses from a big basket near me, and kept cool and jolly, and enjoyed it all.

Encouraging a Daughter's Self-Renewal

‒‒‒‒‒‒

Bronson Alcott and his daughter Anna Alcott

Bronson Alcott was a prominent New England philosopher and social reformer of the mid-nineteenth century. His notable friends included Ralph Waldo Emerson, Margaret Fuller, and Henry David Thoreau. Alcott is also famous as the father of Louisa May Alcott, who wrote *Little Women* and other popular novels. He created the Temple School in Boston, devoted to spiritual development, and also helped found several utopian communes.

Visiting in Boston in March 1839, Bronson Alcott sent this letter to his daughter Anna. Talented in acting, she later became the basis for the character Meg in *Little Women*:

> This is your birthday. You have now lived eight years with your father and mother. Do you want to know how you can be so beautiful and so sweet? It is easy. Only try, with all your

resolution, to mind that which the silent teacher in your breast says to you: that is all.

A birthday is a good time to begin to live anew: throwing away the old habits, as you would old clothes, and never putting them on again. Begin, my daughter, today, and when your next birthday shall come, how glad you will be that you made the resolution. Resolution makes all things new.

Encouraging a Daughter's Writing Ability

❧

Abigail Alcott and her daughter Louisa May Alcott

Abigail May Alcott, mother of the novelist Louisa May Alcott, was born in Boston, in 1800, the youngest of twelve children. Looking back on her youth, she recalled candidly, "My schooling was much interrupted by ill health, but I danced well and at the dancing school, I had for partners some boys who afterwards became eminent. I did not love study, but books were attractive."

At the age of nineteen, Abigail broadened her education with a private tutor in French, Latin, botany, and history. She first met her future husband, the social reformer and philosopher Henry Amos Alcott, at the home of her brother, the Reverend Samuel May. It was apparently love at first sight, for in Abigail's view she had finally met, at age thirty, "the only being whom I ever loved as companionable."

They raised four daughters, including Louisa May Alcott, the famed author of *Little Women* and other works.

In November 1842, little Louisa received this letter from her mother:

> Your tenth birthday has arrived. May it be a happy one, and on each returning birthday may you feel new strength and resolution to be gentle with sisters, obedient to parents, loving to everyone, and happy in yourself.
>
> I give you the pencil case I promised, for I have observed that you are fond of writing, and wish to encourage the habit.
>
> Go on trying, dear, and each day it will be easier to be and do good. You must help yourself, for the cause of your little troubles is in yourself, and only patience and courage will make you what mother prays to see you: her good and happy girl.

Enhancing A Son's Learning

<hr />

Kenneth Grahame and his son, Alastair

Kenneth Grahame is best known today as author of *The Wind in the Willows,* the beloved children's novel chronicling the adventures of Toad and other animal characters. Grahame was the distinguished secretary to the Bank of England, but with his only child, Alistair, he participated in a very different, entertaining, and imaginative world.

In May 1907, Grahame wrote his four-year-old son these words, which formed the basis of *The Wind in the Willows:*

> This is a birthday letter to wish you many happy returns of the day. I wish we could have been together, but we shall meet again soon and then we will have treats. I have sent you two picture books, one about Brer Rabbit, from Daddy, and one about other animals, from Mummy. And we have sent you a boat, painted red, with mast and sails to sail in the round pond by the

windmill, and Mummy has sent you a boat-hook to catch it when it comes ashore. Also Mummy has sent you some sandtoys to play in the sand with, and a card game.

Have you heard about the toad? He was never taken prisoner by the brigands at all. It was all a horrid, low trick of his. He wrote that letter himself: the letter saying that a hundred pounds must be put in the hollow tree. And he got out of the window early one morning and went off to a town called Buggleton and went to the Red Lion Hotel, and there he found a party that had just motored down from London, and while they were having breakfast he went into the stableyard and found their motor car, and went off in it without even saying Poop-poop! And now he has vanished and everyone is looking for him, including the police. I fear he is a bad, low animal.

Enjoying a Getaway with One's Husband

Margaret Mitchell and her husband, John Marsh

Gone With the Wind, which won the Pulitzer Prize in 1937 and was made two years later into a remarkably popular movie, reflected author Margaret Mitchell's origins and milieu. Born in 1900 to a fifth-generation Georgian, she worked as a reporter for the *Atlanta Journal* before resigning in 1926 to begin writing what would become her only full-length book. It took nine years for her to find a publisher and see the novel's release, but it sold a million copies within its first six months.

Set in Civil War and Reconstructionist Georgia, *Gone With the Wind* became an American entertainment phenomenon, offering such memorable characters as the beautiful Scarlett O'Hara and dastardly Rhett Butler. Though Mitchell maintained a voluminous correspondence, she never published another novel and died tragically in a car accident at the age of forty-nine.

As Marianne Walker related in *Margaret Mitchell and John Marsh: The Love Story Behind Gone With the Wind*:

The Marshes celebrated Peggy's thirty-sixth birthday by slipping away for a weekend to Sea Island, their favorite resort on the Georgia coast. John registered them as "Mr. and Mrs. John Munnerlyn," a pseudonym they started using whenever they traveled. The hotel was beautiful and heavenly quiet, and about Sea Island she wrote, "There is no place in the world so still."

They slept late each morning and had hearty breakfasts of hot coffee and fresh fruit, eggs, buttered grits, and bacon served in their room every day. In the afternoons, they took leisurely drives "through long avenues of enormous trees with yards of Spanish moss hanging down." John wished that they could stay in that isolated spot for two or three months so that she could get the rest and relaxation she needed.

But that was not possible. Just a few hours before they were ready to leave, someone recognized Peggy and shouted to her. She waved back, and then she and John scurried off in the opposite direction, giggling as they made a secret exit from the hotel. Complaining about having to talk to so many people she did not want to talk to, she asked, "Why is it that the attractive people you want to catch are so elusive and the time stealers are with us always?"

Enjoying Foreign Travel

Babe Ruth

Babe Ruth was America's first great home-run hitter, and perhaps its first major sports celebrity as well. After starting his career with the Baltimore Orioles, and then becoming an acclaimed pitcher for the Boston Red Sox, Ruth joined the New York Yankees in 1920. He became so popular with fans that Yankee Stadium, which opened in 1923, was dubbed "The House That Ruth Built." Ruth set many batting records during his fourteen-year career with the Yankees, but was released after the 1934 season. He ended his playing career in 1935 with the Boston Braves, and in the final game, hit three home runs. The following year, Ruth became one of the first five players to be inducted into the National Baseball Hall of Fame.

In *Babe: The Legend Comes to Life,* Robert Creamer recounted Ruth's trip around the world during the winter of 1936:

Babe was much happier in England, the last stop before sailing home. He celebrated his forty-first birthday the day he arrived; the famous birth certificate saying he was a year younger than he had always thought had been unearthed the previous September when Babe was getting ready for the trip, but he had ignored it.

Everyone in London seemed to know who he was. Alan Fairfax, a former Australian cricketer, took him to an indoor cricket pitch and taught him the rudiments of the game. Babe tried to bat cricket style, but shifted to his baseball stance and hit beautifully. "It's a better game than I thought," he said. Fairfax quipped: "I wish I could have him for a fortnight. I'd make the world's greatest cricket batsman out of him."

Paul Tillich

German-born Paul Tillich had a huge impact on twentieth century philosophy and theology. His works on life's meaning included *The Courage to Be, Dynamics of Faith*, and *The Eternal Now*. Tillich was dismissed for political reasons from his professorship at the University of Frankfurt when Hitler took power over Germany in 1933 and immediately emigrated to the United States. He taught first at Union Theological Seminary in New York, then at Harvard University, and, finally, at the University of Chicago.

In his intriguing *Travel Diary: 1936, Between Two Worlds,* Tillich recounted his fiftieth birthday while visiting friends near scenic Locarno, Switzerland:

I wake up at a quarter to seven. Suddenly, at seven, a four-part chorus, "The golden sun, man has no goodness greater than this . . ." I bawl without restraint and beg Hermann not to let anyone come in. Twenty years ago, the regimental band played "Full thirty years old are you now" on the dot of seven, just like today. This is too much. And once again, the people I love best are far away.

Get up. Breakfast with fifty red candles and one big yellow life-light whose streams of lava feed the smaller lights and keep them going. By and by, they all burn holes into the black soil on an old serving tray which begins to look like an astronomer's map. Cake, flowers. Everyone has joined in the singing; I throw them all out and read my birthday letters.

The women are in the kitchen, preparing lunch which has been provided by the Berks and will be served in the garden of the Villa Voltata. A birthday spread with much Asti Spumante, sandwiches and fruit, beneath a pear tree. Behind the bushes, luncheon music from one of the cafes, provided by Hermann.... Later, general nap time, then coffee, and off to the lake by motorboat. We have a great swim in indescribable water. At six, everyone assembles on my balcony for a discussion. Subject: the idea of progress. I initiate the discussion from the American viewpoint....

Still later, a great dinner table at Quattrino's. The best *vino nostrano, pollo amato;* after dinner, renewed discussion. I come out too strongly against Hermann. We dance at the Taverna. I go to bed very late, and very much moved by torrents of love.

Enjoying Old Age

Frank Laubach

Dubbed "Mr. Literacy" by *Time* magazine, Dr. Frank Laubach pioneered the adult literacy movement. Through his efforts as an educator, communicator, and organizer, millions of poor and disenfranchised people around the globe have been empowered to better their lives through literacy. After serving in 1930 as a missionary among the Maranao tribe in the Philippines, Laubach became convinced that literacy was essential for social improvement and change. Over the next forty years, he visited 103 countries in an attempt to bring literacy to the "silent billion."

In 1964 Laubach authored this humorous piece, entitled *Life Begins at 80* (subsequently reprinted in *The Best of Ann Landers*):

I have good news for you. The first 80 years are the hardest. The second 80 are a succession of birthday parties.

Once you reach 80, everyone wants to carry your baggage and help you up the steps. If you forget your name or anybody else's name, or an appointment, or your own telephone number, or promise to be three places at the same time, or can't remember how many grandchildren you have, you need only explain that you are 80.

Being 80 is a lot better than being 70. At 70 people are mad at you for everything. At 80 you have a perfect excuse no matter what you do. If you act foolishly, it's your second childhood. Everybody is looking for symptoms of softening of the brain.

Being 70 is no fun at all. At that age they expect you to retire to a house in Florida and complain about your arthritis (they used to call it lumbago) and you ask everybody to stop mumbling because you can't understand them. (Actually your hearing is about 50 percent gone.)

If you survive until you are 80, everybody is surprised that you are still alive. They treat you with respect just for having lived so long. Actually they seem surprised that you can walk and talk sensibly.

So, please, folks, try to make it to 80. It's the best time of life. People forgive you for anything. If you ask me, life begins at 80.

Experiencing Life as a Gift

※※※

Thomas Merton

"The things I thought were so important—because of the effort I put into them—have turned out to be of small value. And the things I never thought about: the things I was never able to either measure or to expect, were the things that mattered," revealed Thomas Merton, one of America's most important religious thinkers of the past half century.

A Roman Catholic monk who lived in a Trappist monastery in Kentucky, Merton was a prolific writer whose over forty books include *The Seven Storey Mountain,* his famous, autobiographical work, and *Faith and Violence, New Seeds of Contemplation,* and *Conjectures of an Innocent Bystander*. In later life, Merton became fascinated by Buddhism and Zen philosophy, and provocatively related such teachings to classic Western spirituality.

Merton's posthumously published journal, *A Search for Solitude,* contained this January 1960 entry:

I never thought to have had such a thing as a forty-fifth birthday. Why was I always half-convinced I would die young? Perhaps a kind of superstition—the fear of admitting a hope of life which, if admitted, might have to be dashed. But now "I have lived" a fair span of life, and whether or not the fact be important, nothing can alter it. It is certain, infallible—even though that too is only a kind of dream.

Life is a gift I am glad of, and I do not curse the day when I was born. On the contrary, if I had never been born, I would never have had friends to love and to be loved by, never have made mistakes to learn from, never have seen new countries. As for what I may have suffered, it is inconsequential and indeed part of the great good which life has been and will, I hope, continue to be.

Because, after all, as I suddenly realize, 45 is still young.

William Butler Yeats

"Tread softly because you tread on my dreams," wrote William Butler Yeats, considered one of the greatest English-language poets of the past century. Leader of the Irish Literary Renaissance in the early 1900s, Yeats drew from legend, occultism, and personal mystical experience to fashion a new vision of human existence in the modern world. His works include *The Tower, The Wild Swans at Coole,* and *The Wind Among the Reeds.* In 1922, Yeats became a senator of the Irish Free State after the Anglo-Irish war, and the following year, he received the Nobel Prize for literature.

Many of Yeats' evocative poems focus on individual spirituality and inner growth against the backdrop of passing time. In his celebrated collection *The Winding Stair and Other Poems,* published in 1933, Yeats recalled in a poem entitled "Vacillation":

> My fiftieth year had come and gone,
> I sat, a solitary man,
> In a crowded London shop,
> An open book and empty cup
> On the marble table-top.
>
> While on the shop and street I gazed
> My body of a sudden blazed;
> And twenty minutes more or less
> It seemed, so great, my happiness,
> That I was blessed and could bless.

Experiencing Youthful Rebellion

Abraham Maslow

Abraham Maslow, considered to be among the world's most important psychological thinkers of the past half-century, is acclaimed for his insights into human nature and motivation. He was born to Russian-Jewish parents in the early twentieth century and grew up in Brooklyn, New York. During his childhood, "Abe" (as everyone called him) was exposed to no formal Jewish education at all. He was bound, therefore, to experience the bar mitzvah (religious confirmation at age thirteen) as empty—particularly when he was required to memorize words he did not understand.

But even more painful was the speech Abe was expected to give praising his parents for their selfless devotion to him. To publicly mouth words that contradicted his strongest emotions—he and his mother had a horrible relationship—was unbearable. In describing what religion had meant to him in his early years, Maslow decades later recollected:

I was taught by rote certain Hebrew passages. I wasn't interested in Hebrew, so I didn't care to learn the language at all. I was just trudging through this task, which was imposed upon me, and then I was supposed to make a speech. . . . They just picked them out of books that were sold in stationery stores, and they always started, "My dear mother and father," and I had to make this speech, and it was just terrible.

And then, in the middle of the speech, as I started talking about the blessing of my dear mother—you were supposed to turn to your mother and say: "My dear mother, to whom I owe my life, and to whom I owe my upbringing," and "to whom I owe this, that, and the other thing," and "How I love you for it"—I burst into tears and fled, just ran away, because the whole thing was so hypocritical I couldn't stand it.

Ironically, young Maslow's disgust was misinterpreted by its chief witness. As her oldest son bolted in tears from the synagogue podium, Rose Maslow triumphantly turned to the assembled relatives and announced, "You see! He loves me so much he can't even express the words!" She thought, or perhaps wanted the others to think, that he had been overcome by feelings of devotion.

Expressing Admiration to a Friend

Leonard Bernstein and his friend Stephen Sondheim

Born in New York City, songwriter Stephen Sondheim showed prodigious talent at an early age. Such celebrated musicals as *Sweeney Todd, A Funny Thing Happened to Me On the Way to the Forum*, and *A Little Night Music*—with its haunting song "Send in the Clowns"—owe their existence to his lyricism.

After graduating with honors from Williams College in 1950, Sondheim studied under the composer Milton Babbitt and began writing television scripts and incidental Broadway show music in his early twenties. In 1956, he was chosen to collaborate with Leonard Bernstein on the new Broadway musical *West Side Story*.

In an anthology called *Findings,* Bernstein included this affectionate acrostic written in March 1957 for his friend's twenty-seventh birthday:

Stephen Sondheim is a maker and solver of puzzles:
The jigsaw of his mind, the crosswords of creation, and
  especially the cryptologies of the heart.
Puzzle-poet of word and note, puzzled by some, puzzling to
  others,
He will (may), like his work-puzzle, inch apart, just
Enough to reveal the delicate cracks between:
Next moment the pieces magnetize and spring together with
  jolting rightness.

Stephen Sondheim loves Christmas: not
Only for the joy of giving the precisely definitive gift,
Not, certainly, for the getting; but for the ritual,
Decembral restatement of warmth and remembrance.
He is compulsively loyal,
Even to friends who are disloyal to one another, which is
  loyalty
Indeed. Puzzler, poet, friend, riddle,
Musician.

Arnold Zweig and his friend Sigmund Freud

A German novelist and dramatist some thirty years Sigmund Freud's
junior, Arnold Zweig is best known for his trilogy of novels *Education*

Before Verdun, The Case of Sergeant Grischa, and *The Crowning of a King.* Soon after Hitler came to power in Germany, Zweig emigrated to the Holy Land, where he continued to write actively.

In May 1934, Zweig was living in scenic Haifa when he sent this letter of admiration to Freud on his seventy-eighth birthday:

This is to reach you on May 6th and congratulate you with a bow and a kiss on the hand, as grandchildren used to do in days gone by. And so that it may not come empty-handed, it brings with it the first draft of a plan that I would like to start soon: a novel about Nietzche's madness. You know that ever since the end of the War, I have turned away bitterly from this idol of my youth. . . .

Now, after many years, I have come close to him again, because in you I recognized the man who had carried out all that Nietzche first dreamed of: who has given new life to the world of antiquity, who has reversed old values . . . who has given new names to human instincts and has contributed a critique of the course of civilization as we know it. But you have avoided all his distortions and follies, just because you invented analysis and not Zarathustra.

Expressing Career Satisfaction to a Friend

Philip Larkin and his friend Alan Pringle

Philip Larkin was a prize-winning English novelist and poet. His works include *Jill, High Windows,* and *In the Grip of Light*. Larkin showed literary talent at an early age, and after graduating from Oxford in 1943, took a position as assistant librarian at the University College of Leicester.

Larkin quickly wrote two books, a novel, and a collection of poems, but gaining true recognition proved more difficult than he had initially imagined. It was soon after the well-received appearance of his second novel, *A Girl in Winter,* that he offered these joyful sentiments in August 1947 to his publisher and friend Alan Pringle:

> I am very pleased by your kind letter which arrived aptly today, my twenty-fifth birthday. It's comforting to think that *A*

Girl in Winter has justified its publication and has not left you with any unsalable copies cluttering up your store-rooms (perhaps that situation does not occur these days, though). As regards a reprint, I do still see copies hanging about in shops, and I suppose if there were a widespread demand still, those copies would go.

What encourages me most is the idea that what I enjoy writing other people are prepared to risk reading. In the last few days, I have made an infinitely tentative start on another book: I hope to proceed with it unhurriedly for the next year or two, cheered by the fate of the first.

John Steinbeck and his friend Elizabeth Otis

John Steinbeck is best known for his powerful novels including *Of Mice and Men* and *The Grapes of Wrath*. Born in Salinas, California, he struggled until his mid-thirties in such odd jobs as bricklaying before gaining the attention of the literary world with his fourth novel, *Tortilla Flat,* published in 1942. Early in his writing career, Steinbeck became friendly with literary agent Elizabeth Otis in New York City. Their relationship deepened over the years. In August 1951, Steinbeck shared his feelings about his then-novel-in-progress, *East of Eden*. As Steinbeck accurately sensed it would be greeted with acclaim:

> The birthday is over and it was a humdinger and I think [my wife] Elaine was happy with it. I am going to leave birthday-telling to Elaine. I worked into Sunday and finished Book III so that now I have just one more book in this novel. And I start it after a rest and a change which is good because it is different from the rest, in time, pace, and everything.
>
> I am still not bored with it. And I should be by this time. But it is, if anything, more alive to me than ever. And I feel a hugeness in my chest out of which I hope pigmies do not come. The last book will be between 70 and 80 thousand words, or roughly two more months of work if I am lucky. So it is still on schedule even though I have tried to keep schedule out of it. We have just one more month here. It looks now as though Way might be able come, which will make us very happy. And I'll have to get ready for a whole new kind of life when this book is done (if I am to live at all) because with *East of Eden* one part of my life is finished. But even that is fun to contemplate.

It is a very big book, Elizabeth. I don't know whether or not it is very good, but I am sure it is the very best and purest of which I am capable, given my faults and virtues and training. It is going down on paper and there are no complaints or excuses. It's all I have ever learned, and it is really good to be out on this gigantic limb. I can't say—"I might have done better"—because I mightn't.

And I'm glad.

Expressing Fatherly Admiration

※※※

Isaac D'Israeli and his son Benjamin Disraeli

Benjamin Disraeli was among the most important British political leaders of the nineteenth century. He twice served as Great Britain's prime minister, the first person of Jewish ancestry to attain this post. Among the achievements of Disraeli's government was an improvement in living conditions and the implementation of many measures affecting health, housing, working conditions, and the environment. He also wrote several novels, including *Coningsby, Sybil,* and *Tancred*.

Isaac D'Israeli, Benjamin's father, was a well-known London author, scion to a wealthy merchant family. He had his son baptized at the age of thirteen into the Church of England. Just before turning thirty-one in December 1835, Disraeli had published a major essay entitled *A Vindication of the English Constitution*. His father then sent this supportive letter:

Your vulgar birthday was, it seems, last Monday, but your noble political birth has occurred this week, and truly, like the fable of old, you have issued into existence armed in the full panoply of the highest wisdom. You have now a positive name and a being in the great political world, which you had not ten days ago. It is for you to preserve the wide reputation which I am positive is now secured. I never doubted your powers—they were not latent to me. With more management on your side they would have been acknowledged long ere now universally.

You never wanted for genius, but it was apt in its fullness to run over.

You have acquired what many a genius never could—a perfect style—and that's a pickle which will preserve even matter less valuable than what you, I doubt not, will always afford the world. You have rejected the curt and flashy diction which betrayed perpetual effort.... All that now remains for you to do is to register "a vow in heaven" that you will never write anything inferior to what you have now written, and never to write but on a subject which may call forth all your energies.

Should you ever succeed in getting into Parliament I will know that your moral intrepidity and your rapid combinations of ideas will throw out many "a Vindication" in the brilliance and irresistible force of your effusions.

Benjamin Latrobe and his son, John

Benjamin Latrobe was architect and engineer of the Capitol in Washington and of various projects for the proper use and control of America's great rivers. While planning flood control of the Mississippi in May 1819, he sent this letter from New Orleans to his son, John, who was turning sixteen at West Point. In later years, John would achieve success as an inventor, attorney for several railroad firms, and philanthropist:

At the table at which I am sitting to write to you, and to congratulate myself on occasion of his birthday that I have a son such as you, I presume that my head is at least four feet below the present level of the water in the Mississippi, while yours is raised two or three hundred feet above the tide. You will be pleased to observe that I am congratulating myself in the first instance, but also most sincerely congratulate you that you are now sixteen, and have hitherto given nothing but pleasure and satisfaction to your parents.

May God preserve you, my dear boy, what you now are: an honest, upright and generous being, conscious of the errors of his own heart and head, and indulgent to those of his fellow beings—never looking for his own gratifications in the injury done to others, but always making self subordinate to humanity, to friendship and to justice....

I am glad that you have taken seriously to the study of history. Gibbon's work will explain my motives for detesting dogmatic theology. But all history is a thing of misrepresentations, or absolute falsehoods, excepting in respect to great leading facts and events. Nothing, however, is so necessary to be known by a gentleman. Otherwise, a man may be apt to act one of the characters of your sporting clerk on the stage of real life....

You see how old Daddies will preach.

Expressing Love to a Friend

※→←※→←※

Rachel Carson and her friend Dorothy Freeman

As the author of such environmental classics as *The Sea Around Us* and *Silent Spring,* marine biologist Rachel Carson enjoyed both popularity and influence in her life. She was born in the rural western Pennsylvania town of Springdale, graduated with degrees from Johns Hopkins University, and began her career with the U.S. Bureau of Fisheries in the mid-1930s. Carson won widespread praise for her warnings about ecological pollution and for the clarity of her writing style.

In an introduction to *The Silent Spring,* then Vice President Al Gore commented that, "Rachel Carson's book offers undeniable proof that the power of an idea can be far greater than the power of politicians. In 1962, when [this book] was first published, 'environment' was not even an entry in the vocabulary of public policy."

Among Carson's closest friends was Dorothy Freeman, nine years her senior and a former high school teacher, agricultural outreach worker, and business executive in the Boston area. The two women met while vacationing with their families in Maine during the early 1950s. Both were married and enjoyed children. They shared a love for nature, literature, and the arts, and corresponded actively—and intimately—over the ensuing years. At the very outset, they felt themselves as "kindred spirits," and only a short while after they had first met, Rachel wrote, "It seems as though I had known you for years instead of weeks, for time doesn't matter when two people think and feel in the same way about so many things."

In June 1956, Carson offered these sentiments to her beloved Dorothy Freeman, who was turning fifty-eight:

> For your birthday, this is to tell you—as if you didn't know—how dearly and tenderly I love you. You have come to occupy a place in my life that no one else could fill, and it is strange now to contemplate all the empty years when you weren't there. But perhaps we shouldn't regret those years—perhaps instead we should just give ourselves over to wonder and gratitude that a friendship so satisfying and so full of joy and beauty could come to each of us in the middle years—when, perhaps, we need it most!
>
> Darling, do you know how wonderful it is to have you? I hope you do.

Mary Haskell and her friend Kahlil Gibran

Mary Haskell, an innovative Boston educator, was Kahlil Gibran's closest friend and benefactor. Ten years his senior, she discovered Gibran's artistic talent in 1904 while visiting the painting studio of a mutual acquaintance. She shared his mystical philosophy and supported him financially throughout his life as an artist and writer in New York City's Greenwich Village.

Upon the occasion of Gibran's twenty-ninth birthday, in January 1912, Haskell sent him this letter:

> Thanks to the *bon Dieu* who gave you to your mother twenty-nine years ago—and one year ago drew you and me nearer together.
>
> I've wept a little over these spirit-tenanted walls, and as yet have not touched them chiefly because my finger tips seem to shed tears at the thought of touching those places. It's been a priceless time, with them in the house, Kahlil.
>
> You and the spring-floods of your new life with their power and strangeness and devastations and the passion of their lover to have the Earth drink them—Ach! It's so natural to think of you, sometimes so hard to write! All I am ever finally impelled to say,

rather than not say, to you of yourself seems resolvable into, "Kahil, you are in my heart—you are in my heart, Kahil." When I look back over the years, it seems always to have been that—with changes only of depth and heat of your heart-place.

Expressing Love to One's Fiancé

Rosa Ferrucci and her fiancé, Gaetano

Rosa Ferrucci was an Italian writer and mystic. Her mother was a poet and translator into English of Ferrucci's letters to her fiancé Gaetano, who courted her devotedly. She died before the marriage could take place the following year. On the occasion of her twenty-fifth birthday in June 1856, Rosa sent him this letter:

> I thank you for your kind intention to come to Pisa on Wednesday. Although my birthday is always a solemn and joyous event, I shall regard it as more sacred than ever, being under a sense of deeper gratitude to God, and feeling that I must thank him for all the favors which he has heaped on me all my life and particularly of late. . . .
>
> I am not ready to marry you at once, because, however much

I love you, I do not wish to experience now the pain that will surely be mine when I leave my parental home.

I would be willing to make it eleven months instead of fifteen and I assure you that this would be a real proof of affection, for the sacrifice of four months of intimate life with the most affectionate of mothers is a supreme one. Nevertheless, I am willing to make it for your sake.

Expressing Love to One's Grandmother

Prince Wilhelm II of Prussia and his grandmother,
Queen Victoria

Queen Victoria was the devoted mother of nine children and a doting grandmother. Her oldest child, Victoria Adelaide Mary Louise (nicknamed "Vicky") married Prince Friedrich Wilhelm I of Prussia when she was seventeen in 1857. He became emperor of Prussia, but died of throat cancer three months after ascending to the throne. Vicky had seven children, the eldest of whom, Wilhelm II, eventually served as Prussia's emperor.

In May 1868, little Wilhelm II sent Britain's celebrated Queen this letter on her forty-ninth birthday:

> I hope you will be quite well to enjoy your birthday. I wish I were near you to congratulate you and to kiss your hand. It is so long since I have seen you, dear Grandmama. We have a large

mast. It is the foremast of the *Hela*. I went up three times on the foretop with Captain von Dresky. The whole length and breadth of the ship is marked out on the ground. We play in it, and about it, and enjoy ourselves famously.

I am now learning Latin. I like it and hope it will please you to hear this. I have so much to do. I beg leave to kiss your hand, remaining with all love and respect your most dutiful, obedient and affectionate grandson.

Expressing Romantic Passion to a Friend

Aline Bernstein and her friend Thomas Wolfe

When Aline Bernstein and Thomas Wolfe first met, the writer was twenty-five and she was forty-four. He was a struggling unknown from Asheville, North Carolina, and she was a successful stage and costume designer who provided him with the financial, emotional, and literary support to finish *You Can't Go Home Again*.

With Bernstein working in New York City theaters and Wolfe writing in Europe, the two were often separated for long periods of time. Their geographic distance and age differences did not allow for a strong relationship, and by early 1931, Wolfe tried to end their six-year involvement completely. However, Bernstein continued to write him. In September 1933, while living in suburban Armonk, New York, she sent this letter:

> I have lost track of how many years ago we met, and last lunched together on your birthday, but I have not forgotten, and

I will carry to my death, the mark you left upon me and my deep love for you. It will never lessen, I will never change. I do not know whether you have the slightest interest in me, but this time since we finally parted has been a terrible and wonderful time. I have conquered myself, my outer self, and still preserved the treasure of my love. I am not in constant pain, and I know now that I must never see you again, that my future companionship with you must be in my mind and heart. In spite of all the black and dreadful years I have spent, I realize the beautiful thing that happened to me, that you and the way I loved you has released such wonder in my whole being.

I have seen through you, through your touch upon me, a world that was dormant before. Have you seen a boy release homing pigeons from a cage? One day coming to see you in Brooklyn, I watched that on a roof, and thought then how like it was to my own state with you. I wish for your happiness and success. I wish that I understood better what came between us to destroy whatever good I held for you. I think you can look down to the very center of yourself, and find beneath the hate for me, just one drop of pure love. God bless you, God help you to use your genius. I thought that I could. I have the utmost faith in your greatness, and I send you, on this birthday [of yours], my whole heart of love.

Margaret Fuller and her friend James Nathan

Margaret Fuller was a celebrated American journalist and social reformer of the mid-nineteenth century. Born in Cambridgeport near Boston, she became a teacher affiliated with the transcendentalist movement headed by Ralph Waldo Emerson and through his influence assumed editorship of *The Dial* in 1840. Soon after, Fuller became literary critic on Horace Greeley's newspaper, *The New York Tribune*. In this position, she encouraged new American writers and crusaded for social reforms including women's rights. Her books included *Papers on Literature and Art* and *Woman in the Nineteenth Century*. As America's first woman foreign correspondent, Fuller was well received in English and French literary circles.

On her thirty-fifth birthday in May 1845, Fuller sent this letter to James Nathan, a talented musician and writer with whom she had fallen in love:

I do not, just now, find anything to write: the fact of an approaching separation presses on my mind and makes me unable to make the best use of the hours that remain.

I will therefore borrow from the past. Many little things have made me feel as if there had been a gradual and divinely-moved preparation for our meeting. Today, I took out of the portfolio some leaves written last autumn among the mountains and found these lines which will impress you from their consonance, in some respects, with what you have since uttered to me. Many such things I write down: they seem dictated to me, and are not understood fully at the time. They are of the things which are received mystically long before they are appreciated intellectually.

Perhaps you had better destroy them, not now, for you will hardly be at leisure for them yet. But sometime, when you feel ready, as they are so intimately personal. . . .

I am not well. You cannot bend your mind on me now. I know it is not because you love me less, but because there are necessarily so many things, at present, to distract. But I feel it. The strength that was only given is gone. Or rather, it was not given, only lent, but you would have given it if you could, I know.

Gustave Flaubert and his friend Louise Colet

One of the most significant French novelists in history was Gustave Flaubert. *Madame Bovary,* with its vivid, romantic outlook and written with a literary style embracing realism, is undoubtedly his most famous work. Its sensual subject matter, about social life in a Normandy village, generated great controversy in his time. Critics often attacked Flaubert for his licentious novels.

For several years, Flaubert carried on a love affair with Louise Colet, a beautiful and seductive poet with many romances. Colet was twelve years Flaubert's senior when they first met in 1846, and served as a partial model for his character Madame Bovary. In December 1852, Flaubert sent Colet this impassioned letter:

> I begin by devouring you with kisses, for I am transported with joy. Your letter of this morning has lifted a terrible weight from my heart.... For three weeks, I have been suffering horribly from worry, and have not stopped thinking of you a second—but in a way that has been scarcely agreeable. I should need a whole book to develop my feelings in a comprehensible manner....
>
> I also had a superstitious thought. Tomorrow, I shall be thirty-one. I have just passed that fatal thirtieth year, the year that ranks a man. It is the age when a man takes his future shape, settles down, marries, chooses a trade. There are few people who do not become bourgeois at thirty. [I do not wish to be] confined within those ordinary ways of living.

The day is fine, the sun is shining on the river. At this moment, a brig is passing with all sails unfurled. My window is open, my fire blazing. Adieu! I love you more than ever, and I kiss you to suffocation in honor of my birthday.

Arthur Henry Hallam and his friend Emily Tennyson

Arthur Henry Hallam, a brilliant young Victorian writer, is known today as poet Alfred, Lord Tennyson's closest and most influential friend. During their four years of intense acquaintanceship, Hallam met Alfred's sister Emily in Somersby and fell passionately in love with her. The two became engaged, but their anticipated marriage never took place due to Hallam's tragic death from illness at the age of twenty-two.

In October 1832, he sent Emily this romantic letter on the occasion of her reaching majority age:

You are so dear and good a creature, you have had so much to suffer, your tender frame is so susceptible to agitating impressions from memory and imagination, that I ought to deal with you delicately, as with a trembling flower, or a being composed of subtler elements than common earth. Yesterday, I read over the greatest part of your letters to me. They filled me with comfort and a strange, melancholy joy.

It is now three years since you arose upon my life like a star. At first the beams were clear but distant; their brightness and their warmth have been increasing ever, but they have not yet reached their meridian and I yearn for the hour of their fullness with impetuousness, believing hope.

Can you wonder that the idea of your birthday is a cherished idea for me? Every birthday, every signal and landmark in the flood of Time brings me nearer to the great object for which I live. . . . that luminous region [of your lasting companionship]. You are twenty-one and have now escaped from the "durance vile" of guardianship.

I have no time to write more, as the post is now going out. May the Merciful God bless you for ever and ever, and yield you a long succession of years, happier than any you have yet known, and rich in perpetual consolations and delights.

Alfred, Lord Tennyson and his friend "Maud"

Alfred, Lord Tennyson was England's most popular poet of the Victorian era. He succeeded William Wordsworth in 1850 to serve as poet laureate of Great Britain. Shunning public life, Tennyson lived quietly in his country homes at Farringford on the Isle of Wight and Aldworth in Surrey. Among his closest friends was Arthur Henry Hallam, featured earlier in this book, who courted Tennyson's sister Emily.

Tennyson's lifelong fascination with legendary King Arthur of Camelot led to his most ambitious work, *Idylls of the King,* and such beautifully lyrical, tender poems as "The Lady of Shalott." His famous love poem "Maud" contained these birthday-related sentiments:

> Ah, what shall I be at fifty,
>   Should Nature keep me alive,
> If I find the world so bitter
>   When I am but twenty-five?
> Yet, if she were not a cheat,
>   If Maud were all that she seemed.
> And her smile were all that I dreamed?
>   Then the world were not so bitter
> But a smile could make it sweet. . . .
>
> I have played with her when a child;
>   She remembers it now we meet.
> Ah, well, well, well, I *may* be beguiled
>   By some coquettish deceit.

Yet, if she were not cheat,
   And Maud was all that she seemed,
And her smile had all that I dreamed,
   Then the world were not so bitter
But a smile could make it sweet.

Finding One's Vocation

Madeleine L'Engle

Madeleine L'Engle is the author of more than forty-five books for all ages, including the beloved children's fantasy, *A Wrinkle in Time.* She has won numerous awards for both fiction and nonfiction and lectures to civic, educational, and religious groups on her literary themes. An only child growing up in 1920s New York City, L'Engle was exposed to much literature and culture. After touring briefly as a professional actress, she devoted herself full-time to writing and raising a large family in rural Connecticut.

In a free-wheeling memoir entitled *A Circle of Quiet,* L'Engle shared many insights about personal development and family life. Her book included this powerful reminiscence:

> I didn't dread being forty. I looked forward to it. My thirties had been such a rough decade in so many ways that I was eager for change. Surely, with the new decade, luck would turn.

On my birthday I was, as usual, out in the Tower working on a book. The children were in school. My husband was at work and would be getting the mail. He called, saying, "I'm sorry to have to tell you this on your birthday, but you'd never trust me again if I kept it from you. _____ has rejected *The Lost Innocent*."

This seemed an obvious sign from heaven. I should stop trying to write. All during the decade of my thirties (the world's nineteen-fifties), I went through spasms of guilt because I spent so much time writing, because I wasn't like a good New England housewife and mother. When I scrubbed the kitchen floor, the family cheered. I couldn't make decent pie crust. I always managed to get something red in with the white laundry in the washing machine, so that everybody wore streaky pink underwear. And with all the hours I spent writing, I was still not pulling my own weight financially.

So the rejection on the fortieth birthday seemed an umistakable command: Stop this foolishness and learn to make cherry pie.

I covered the typewriter in a great gesture of renunciation. Then I walked around and around the room, bawling my head off. I was totally, unutterably miserable.

Suddenly, I stopped, because I realized what my subconscious was doing while I was sobbing: my subconscious mind was busy working out a novel about failure.

I uncovered the typewriter. In my journal I recorded this moment of decision, for that's what it was. I had to write. It was not up to me to say I would stop, because I could not. It didn't matter how small or inadequate my talent. If I never had another book published, and it was very clear to me that this was a real possibility, I still had to go on writing.

I'm glad I made this decision in the moment of failure. It's easy to say you're a writer when things are going well. When the decision is made in the abyss, then it is quite clear that it is not one's own decision at all.

Getting Past a Tough Birthday

Norman Corwin

Writer, director, and pioneer producer of radio dramas, Norman Corwin started his career in the 1940s as the head of special projects for the United Nations radio network. Since then, he has produced dozens of highly acclaimed books, stage plays, screenplays, and teleplays. The recipient of many awards and honorary degrees, Corwin celebrated his eighty-sixth birthday in May 1996 by returning to work as a national radio producer.

In an interview published in *The Ageless Spirit* edited by Philip Berman and Connie Goldman, Corwin reminisced:

> I think that the main thing that is to be cherished in growing old is dignity. Being able to do that for yourself and not to be dependent on others. Unfortunately, the attitude in this society is that if you're old, it is over. There are many countries where this

attitude is alien. In the Orient, old people are national trea-sures. . . .

Since I'm on the subject of looking back, I remember now that the toughest birthday I ever faced was my fortieth. It was a big symbol because it said goodbye, goodbye, goodbye to youth. Even in the late thirties, one still clings to the notion that one's a young man. It seemed to me to be calamitous to be forty, until, of course, I considered the alternative. But I think that when one has passed through that age, it's like breaking the sound barrier. One realizes that it's not that bad on the other side. One slowly arrives at an accommodation, and that's part of the maturing process.

Gratitude for Friends

Hans Christian Andersen

Hans Christian Andersen was Denmark's most famous author. His fairy tales are among the most widely read works in world literature, and include *The Ugly Duckling, The Emperor's New Clothes, The Story of a Mother*, and *The Tinder Box*. Many of Andersen's fairy tales have serious moral meanings intended for adults. Growing up in poverty, Andersen was impelled by a passionate love for writing. He earned an early reputation as a playwright and novelist, but achieved enduring fame for his fairy tales, the first collection of which was published in 1835. In later years, his friends included Charles Dickens, Victor Hugo, and composer Franz Liszt.

As recounted by Elias Bredsdorff in *Hans Christian Andersen: The Story of His Life and Work,* the writer's seventieth birthday in April 1875 was celebrated internationally; he lived only four months beyond that joyous event.

The day before his birthday, the royal carriage was sent to fetch him to Amalienborg Castle, where the king bestowed upon him yet another decoration and spoke of the happiness Andersen had brought to all the world's countries. The birthday itself, which Andersen had anticipated with a certain trepidation, began with a reception and ended with an early dinner party at a patron-friend's house. This was followed by a visit to the Royal Theater, where two of Andersen's plays were performed.

"What a wonderful, magnificent day!" he commented in his diary, "and yet, how pitiable is my frail body in carrying all these blessings from God. I could not sleep when I went to bed, but was overwhelmed with thoughts and gratitude."

Among the birthday presents was a special polyglot volume which the learned philologist Villhelm Thomsen had compiled. It comprised Andersen's *Story of a Mother* in fifteen languages. None of the birthday tributes pleased Andersen more than a leading article in the London *Daily News,* however, which extolled him:

"The poet who perhaps touches a wider circle of admirers than any other living man-of-letters, is dear to the children of every European country, and has established his fame in the hearts of future generations. . . . It has been given to Hans Andersen to fashion beings, it may almost be said, of a new kind, to breathe life into the toys of childhood and the forms of antique superstition. The tin soldier, the ugly duckling, the mermaid, the little match girl, are no less real and living in their way than Othello, or Mr. Pickwick, or Helen of Troy.... This Danish poet alone, of all who have labored in this field of nursery legend and childhood fancy, has succeeded in recovering and reproducing the kind of imagination which constructed the old fairy tales."

Honoring Entertainment Achievement

Bob Hope

At ninety-eight years of age, wise-cracking Bob Hope is one of America's oldest active show business performers. Born in London, he moved as a child with his family to Cleveland, and embarked on a vaudeville career in the early 1920s. Hope made his debut on Broadway in 1927, and soon starred in the musical comedy *Roberta*. Hope began starring in both radio and film during the 1930s; his first feature movie was *The Big Broadcast,* in 1938, in which he first sang "Thanks for the Memory"; this song became Hope's theme tune.

Hope has appeared in over fifty films, and has been honored on several occasions by the U.S. Congress and Presidents Kennedy, Carter, and Clinton for his humanitarian efforts. In *The Secret Life of Bob Hope,* biographer Arthur Marx (son of Groucho) recounted:

A high-point in 1978 was Bob Hope's seventy-fifth birthday, on May 29. Like a Polish wedding, the festivities seemed to go on forever, in many different locales.

Actually, it only went on for a couple of days, and of course it was inevitable that the main part of the celebration would wind up as one of Hope's specials for Texaco, over NBC.

That part of the celebration was a collaborative effort involving Hope, network and sponsor. It was to be a three-hour star-studded show performed on the stage of the Kennedy Center in Washington. The concept was that the set was to be "an animated birthday card" featuring some of the glitziest names in show business: Pearl Bailey, Lucille Ball, George Burns, Sammy Davis Jr., Redd Foxx, Elliott Gould, Alan King, Dorothy Lamour, Carol Lawrence, Fred MacMurray, Donny and Marie Osmond, Telly Savalas, George C. Scott, Elizabeth Taylor, Danny Thomas, and John Wayne.

Before the show, Bob and his wife, Dolores, were given a luncheon by a group of congressional wives, and then went to the White House for a reception in the East Room. Some five hundred guests from Washington and Hollywood were gathered to pay tribute . . . Jimmy Carter, the First Lady and daughter Amy were on hand to congratulate Hope. Carter delivered a short speech, which sounded as if it could have been written by Bob's writers:

"I've been in office four hundred and eighty-nine days. Three weeks more and I'll have stayed in the White House as many times as Bob Hope has. Bob has a second career making commercials, but it's not true that he sold Pepsodent to George Washington. We all knew he had wooden teeth. He was a Lemon Pledge man."

The following day, at least twenty Congressmen got up on the floor of the House of Representatives to speak about how Bob Hope was a great American. Jim Wright of Texas got a laugh when he declared, "I would not want to suggest that Bob Hope has been entertaining American troops a long time, but it seems only fair to report that there is no other entertainer who has fan letters from Lexington and Concord."

Honoring the Life of a Role Model

⫸⫷

Jane Addams on George Washington

Born in rural Illinois, the eighth of nine children, Jane Addams was celebrated in her lifetime as a pioneer social worker and advocate for international cooperation. A crusading figure on behalf of Chicago's poor and immigrants, she cofounded Hull House, which became a model community center for impoverished urban neighborhoods throughout the United States and abroad.

In February 1903, Addams was invited to speak at the Union League Club in Chicago. Ostensibly a celebration of George Washington's birthday, her oration moved beyond a remembrance of "Washington, the man" to outline the values and priorities that Addams saw as vital for George Washington's America in the then-new twentieth century:

We meet together upon these birthdays of our great [figures], not only to review their lives, but to revive and cherish our own patriotism. This matter is a difficult task. In the first place, we are prone to think that by merely reciting these great deeds, we get a reflected glory, and that the future is secure to us because the past has been so fine.

In the second place, we are apt to think that we inherit the fine qualities of those great [figures], simply because we have had a common descent and are living in the same territory. . . . It is easy to think only of their great deeds, and not to think enough of their spirit. . . .

If we go back to George Washington and ask what he would be doing were he bearing our burdens now, and facing our problems at this moment, we would, of course, have to study his life bit by bit: his life as a soldier, as a statesman, and as a simple Virginia planter. . . .

First, as a soldier. What is that we admire about the soldier? It certainly is not that he goes into battle; rather, that he has the power of losing his own life for a larger cause, that he holds his personal suffering of no account, that he flings down in the gage of battle his all and says, "I will stand or fall with this cause." That, it seems to me, is the glorious thing we most admire [in

George Washington], and if we're going to preserve that same spirit of the soldier, we will have to found a similar spirit in the civil life of the people, the same pride in civil warfare, the spirit of courage, and the spirit of self-surrender which lies back of this. . . .

Let us say again that the lessons of great [figures] are lost unless they reinforce upon our minds the highest demands which we make upon ourselves; that they are lost unless they drive our sluggish wills forward in the direction of their highest ideals.

Ralph Waldo Emerson on Robert Burns

America's leading nineteenth-century philosopher, Ralph Waldo Emerson, was also a minor poet who recognized the major poetic talent in Scotsman Robert Burns. Although the "low" speech of Burns, written in the Scottish vernacular, kept his reputation from rising to the heights of a Keats or Tennyson, Emerson admiringly saw in him a "poet of the poor" and "of the middle class" who could transform a dialect "unintelligible to all but natives" into a "[language] of fame."

In a public speech in January 1859, Emerson commemorated the centennial of Robert Burns:

Robert Burns, the poet of the middle class, represents in the mind of [humanity] today that great uprising of the middle class against the armed and privileged minorities—that uprising which worked positively in the American and French revolutions, and which, not in governments so much as in education and in social order, has changed the face of the world. In order for this destiny, his birth, breeding, and fortune were low. His organic sentiment was absolute independence, and resting, as it should, on a life of labor.

No [one] existed who could look down upon him. They that looked into his eyes saw that they might look down upon the sky as easily. His muse and his teaching was common sense, joyful, aggressive, irresistible. . . . He is an exceptional genius. The people who care nothing for literature and poetry care for Burns. It was indifferent—they thought who saw him—whether he wrote verse or not; he could have done anything else as well.

Yet how true a poet he is! How many *Bonny Doons* and *John Anderson My Joes,* and *Auld Lang Synes* all around the earth have his verses been applied to! And his love songs still woo and melt the youths and maids, the farm work, the country holiday, the fishing cobble, are still his debtors today. . . .

The memory of Burns—every man's and boy's, every woman's

and girl's—carries snatches of his songs, and can say them by heart, and, what is strangest of all, never learned them from a book, but from mouth to mouth. The wind whispers them, the birds whistle them, the corn, barley, and bulrushes hoarsely rustle them: nay, the music boxes of Geneva are framed and toothed to play them; the hand organs of the Savoyards in all cities repeat them, and the chimes of bells ring them in the spires. They are the property and the solace of humanity.

Stephen Wise on Abraham Lincoln

Stephen Wise was among the most prominent Jewish-American leaders of his time. Born in Hungary, he emigrated to the United States as a child and became a Reform rabbi. As founder of the Free Synagogue of New York in 1907, Wise was an outspoken figure for the immigrant poor and active on behalf of progressive social causes; among his close friends was Louis Brandeis, later to serve as U.S. Supreme Court justice.

Widely known for his oratorical power, Wise attracted large audiences to Carnegie Hall. In his sermons he focused on subjects of popular concern—especially issues that would lead Wise into global politics. In 1936 he became the founder of the World Jewish Congress, an influential organization in the fight against Hitler and Nazism.

In February 1914 Wise delivered a Lincoln's Birthday speech in the Great Emancipator's hometown, Springfield, Illinois:

> We dwell in times of great perplexity and are by beset by far-reaching problems of social, industrial, and political import. We shall not greatly err if upon every occasion we consult the genius in Abraham Lincoln. We shall not falter nor swerve from the path of national righteousness if we live by the moral genius of the great American commoner.
>
> Instead of following Lincoln, we too often strive to make it appear that he is following us. Instead of emulating him, we too often venture to appropriate him. Instead of sitting at his feet as his disciples, and humbly heeding the echoes of his lips, we attribute to him our own petty slogans. . . .
>
> In his lifetime, Lincoln was maligned and traduced, but detraction during [one's] lifetime affords no test of [one's] life value nor offers any forecast of history's verdict. It would almost seem as if the glory of immortality were anticipated in the life of the great by detraction and denial whilst yet they lived. When a Lincoln-like man arises, let us recognize and fitly honor him. There could be no poorer way of honoring the memory of Lincoln than to assume, as we sometimes do, that the race of Lincoln has perished from the earth, and that we shall never look upon his like again.

One way to ensure the passing of the Lincolns is to assume that another Lincoln can nevermore arise. Would we find Lincoln today, we must not seek him in the guise of a rail-splitter, nor as a wielder of the backwoodsman's axe, but as a mighty smiter of wrong in high places and low.

Motivating One's Daughter

※

Otto Frank and his daughter Anne Frank

The Diary of Anne Frank, among the world's most widely read works relating to the Holocaust, is celebrated for vividly depicting a teenage girl's struggle for self-identity. Anne Frank was born in Frankfurt, Germany, and relocated with her family to the Netherlands when Hitler came to power in 1933.

The *Diary* records the two years, between 1942 and 1944, that Anne and her family spent hiding—with the courageous assistance of non-Jewish friends—at a secret office annex in Amsterdam. Acting on an informer's tip, the Nazis deported them to concentration camps.

Only Anne's father, Otto, survived. After the war ended, he learned from family friends that they had found Anne's diary among papers left behind by German secret police. Published in 1947, the *Diary* has been translated into more than thirty languages. It movingly records Anne's assertion that "In spite of everything, I still believe that people are really good at heart." Today the Frank family's hiding place on the Prinsengracht Canal in Amsterdam has become an international museum.

In June 1943, Anne at age fourteen received a birthday poem from her father. After summarizing the family's events during the past year, Otto offered these lines, which Anne found especially stirring:

> Though youngest here, you are no longer small,
>   But life is very hard, since one and all
> Aspire to be your teacher, thus and thus:
>   "We have experience, take a tip from us."
> "We know because we did it long ago."
>   "Elders are always better, you must know."
> At least, that's been the rule since life began!
>   Our personal faults are much too small to scan;
> This makes it easier to criticize
>   The faults of others which seem double size.
> Please bear with us, your parents, for we try
>   To judge you fairly and with sympathy.
> Corrections sometimes take against your will.

Musing to a Friend About Life

❦

Maude Gonne and her friend William Butler Yeats

William Butler Yeats, as described earlier in this book, was one of Ireland's greatest poets and writers. He enjoyed friendships with many brilliant persons in literature and the arts, but among his closest intimates was a little-known Irish nationalist named Maude Gonne who shared his creative, mystical outlook. When Yeats was twenty-three, he fell obsessively in love with her, but Gonne refused to marry him. Nevertheless, the two remained close and corresponded actively for decades—enjoying what he called a "spiritual marriage."

In June 1928, Gonne and Yeats had known each other for nearly forty years when she sent him this letter upon his sixth-third birthday:

> Why should I be offended at the references to me in [your new poem] *Among School Children?* It is very kind. Oh, how you hate old age. Well, so do I. I see no redeeming features in it, but

I, who am more a rebel against humanity than you, rebel less against nature and accept the inevitable, and go with it gently into the unknown. Only against the sordidness and cruelty of small ambitions I fight until the long rest comes. Out of that rest, I believe the Great Mother will refashion beauty and life again. While we sleep, she will work in the stupendous energy of Creation, but until sleep comes, our souls and bodies fight in weariness which is old age. At the awakening, it will be with the glory and joy of youth again.

Philip Larkin and his friend Jim Sutton

Philip Larkin, a prize-winning English novelist and poet, gained wide attention for his second novel, *A Girl in Winter,* published in 1947, on the occasion of his thirty-ninth birthday in August 1962, Larkin offered these pensive words to a friend:

A rather better morning, I took my mother to the hospital on account of her ears, and found lots of interesting magazines to read in the waiting room. She seems to hear better now, so my patience, which has been exercised rather more than before— though still not as much as it ought to have been—has been rewarded. As for myself, I tried hanging on the stairs, and fancy it does me good, though perhaps it's one of these things that feels good when you stop, like physical exercise in general.

Well, this is still my last letter in the thirties, and I can't say I welcome the prospect of going down life's sunless hill, as Thomas Hardy [in his poem *She, to Him*] calls the latter half of life. Looking back on my first forty years, I think what strikes me most is that hardly any of the things that are supposed to happen or be so, do in fact happen, or are so. What little happens or is so isn't at all expected or agreeable. And I don't feel that everything could have been different if only I'd acted differently: to have acted differently I should have needed to have *felt* differently, to have been different, which means going back years and years, out of my lifetime.

In a way, I feel I am still waiting for life to start, for all these that are supposed to occur as a matter of course. This may be a sign of what the *Times* (was it?) calls "second adolescence." Ah well.

Musing Humorously About Birthdays

~~~~~~

H. L. Mencken

"Every failure teaches a person something: to wit, that one will probably fail again," cynically observed America's influential journalist H. L. Mencken. "Anyone who inflicts the human race with ideas must be prepared to see them misunderstood," he likewise remarked on another occasion. Writer, editor, and social critic, Mencken was associated with the *Baltimore Sun* during his long career, but his opinion columns were syndicated widely. He also wrote book reviews for the *Smart Set* magazine and founded the *American Mercury* in 1923, a sophisticated periodical of humor and current events. He was best known for his savage wit and caustic comments about public figures great and small, but he also wrote a three-part autobiography and a monumental study, *The American Language*.

In September 1942, Mencken recorded this terse entry on the occasion of his sixty-second birthday:

The seat of my office chair, in use for 25 years, is wearing out, my office rug is wearing out, and I am wearing out. As the Chinese say, "It is later than you think."

Calvin Trillin

The contemporary writer Calvin Trillin is a prolific essayist and poet, as well as television commentator. He earned a staff position on *The New Yorker,* which he still contributes to regularly—and displays a dry wit on a variety of topics, including public affairs. He was raised in Kansas City, Missouri, and wrote a memoir, *Messages From My Father,* reflecting on his childhood origins and influences.

In his anthology *Too Soon to Tell,* Trillin reminisced satirically about later, adulthood experiences:

> I knew there could be considerable frustration involved in being too young or too old for even things you didn't particularly want to do. I remember when, some years ago, I realized that I was too old to become a New York City Transit Authority patrolman, and found that a blow to my spirits.
>
> For a long time, I had routinely glanced at the Transit Authority Police Department's recruiting advertisements in the

subway. If you were eighteen to twenty-nine years old and had a high school diploma and were in good general health, the ads said, you could apply for a position as a Transit Authority patrolman. One day I was riding home on the subway when I realized that I was too old to apply.

As it happens, I had never had any desire to become a Transit Authority patrolman. Without having given the matter much thought, I knew I'd find it a trial walking around with all that stuff hanging off my belt.

Still, as I told my wife when I got home, even if you don't happen to want to go to the party, it's nice to be invited.

"Don't worry about it," my wife said, "In a couple of years, you're going to be old enough to be President."

As it happens, I didn't want to be President any more than I wanted to be a Transit Authority patrolman.... But what my wife said ... sort of disturbed me. The other way of looking at the situation she had described was this: I was in that awkward period that you go through when you're too old to become a Transit Authority patrolman and too young to be President—a sort of early thirties no-man's land.

That period can be pretty rough on a person. Maybe that's why a lot of people in their early thirties do weird things.

Offering Avuncular Affection

Ogden Nash and his nephew Theodore

Highlighted earlier in this book, Ogden Nash was a prolific, humorous poet long associated with *The New Yorker*. As recounted in *Loving Letters of Ogden Nash*, he showed writing talent at an early age. In July 1914, Ogden was only twelve years old when he penned this saucy letter to his nephew Theodore:

> Permit your old uncle to congratulate you upon your arrival in this world. It's a cold and cruel world sometimes, but at others, it is hot and kind.
> But don't you think it was rather—well, rather selfish, one might say—to break your brother's nose so soon?
> And listen, my boy, if ever they treat you badly down there, just come to your lonesome old uncle and live with him. By the way, what do you look like? And please tell your grandmother that her grandson's uncles and aunt and grandpa want her a good deal more than her grandson does.

Offering Fatherly Confidence

Harry Truman and his daughter, Margaret

Harry Truman's presidency was marked by such historic events as the dropping of the atomic bomb on Japan, the Allied victory in World War II, the opening of the cold war, and the start of the Korean conflict. In the decades since Truman left office in 1953, historians have come to accord him increasing respect. As a father, Truman was extremely close to his only child, Margaret. While serving as U.S. senator in February 1944, he offered her this heartfelt encouragement:

On Thursday, the day after tomorrow, you'll be twenty years old. It doesn't seem possible, but the facts of time make it so. I hope that you have a most happy birthday and that you'll have an unlimited number of them in the future. That, of course, will depend upon you and your circumstances. You first, and then what happens as old Father Time unreels the future.

You must meet contingencies as they arrive and face them squarely. You should have enough of your mother's willpower and strength of character, and your dad's affability to make out.

Pondering the Nature of Time

◆◆◆◆◆

Beatrix Potter

As the creator of Peter Rabbit, Jemima Puddle-Duck, and other animal characters, Beatrix Potter ranks among the most famous children's book writers of all time. Born into a wealthy Middlesex family, she grew up in Victorian England and was educated at home solely by private tutors. With a love for both writing and watercolor painting, Potter began her influential career in her twenties by sending illustrated animal stories to the sick child of a former governess.

These letters about the Flopsey Bunnies, Tom Kitten, Miss Moppet, and their friends were so captivating that Potter decided to publish privately *The Tale of Peter Rabbit,* in 1900. She eventually found a commercial publisher, Frederick Warne & Company, which over thirty years brought out twenty-three of the books that made her famous, including *The Tale of Squirrel Nutkin* and *The Tale of Benjamin Bunny.*

As related by Leslie Linder in *The Journal of Beatrix Potter,* Potter recorded in June 1884 this entry in her secretly coded diary:

Papa has been photographing old Gladstone this morning at Mr. Millais'. The old person is evidently a great talker if once started. Papa said he talked in a set manner as if he were making a speech, but without affection. They kept off politics, of course, and talked about photography. Mr. Gladstone talked of it on a large scale, but not technically: what would it come to, how far would the art be carried, did papa think people would ever be able to photograph in color? Papa thinks the portrait promises very well. There have been three sittings.

I am eighteen today. How time does go. I feel as if I had been going on such a time. How grandma must feel! What funny notions of life I used to have as a child. I often thought of the time when I would be eighteen. It's a queer business. . . .

Elie Wiesel

Elie Wiesel is probably the world's most respected and influential Holocaust survivor and spokesperson. He was born into a religious Jewish-Romanian family in the village of Sighet, and was sixteen years old when deported, along with his entire family and all his Jewish neighbors, to the Auschwitz death camp. His parents and younger sister, Tsipouka, were killed, but young Wiesel was forced into slave labor at Buchenwald, another German death camp. After World War II ended, he settled in France, where he studied at the Sorbonne and became a journalist. In 1956, he relocated to the United States and acquired citizenship.

Wiesel's first novel, *Night,* chronicled his experiences at the hands of the Nazis. It was followed by *Dawn, The Town Beyond the Wall, A Beggar in Jerusalem,* and many other works. In 1985, Wiesel was awarded the U.S. Congressional Gold Medal of Achievement, and the following year, he won the Nobel Peace Prize. Wiesel holds a professorship at Boston University and travels frequently around the globe as a lecturer.

In a fascinating anthology, *Telling the Tale: A Tribute to Elie Wiesel on His Sixty-fifth Birthday,* edited by Harry Cargas, the famed writer in 1991 offered these thoughtful words. They came in response to the question: "With another birthday, it seems appropriate and natural to reflect on time. What does time mean to you as it passes?"

I am not afraid of time. Time to me is a puzzle. It's a vehicle, and I may choose to travel in it, or I may choose to run after it. As for the past itself, strangely—maybe it's not so strange—I think about it more often than then. With every day that passes, I dream about those days and nights [of the Holocaust] more frequently. In a peculiar way, the events that I dream about seem more brutal, more and more tragic. I see people with more clarity than before because now they involve not only the past, but the present as well.

In my dreams, I see persons who are here and who were never there, yet I see them somehow involved with the people who were there. It is not so peculiar on one hand because writing is precisely that. I wrote *Night* because I wanted people who were not part of that period to feel something about that period. Maybe because I feel that even where I have not succeeded—I mean in my books—I have succeeded in my dreams. And my readers, my anonymous readers, whom I know, I see them there.

Praising a Friend's Achievements

❦

Martin Buber and his friend Hermann Hesse

Martin Buber, an influential philosopher of our time, viewed spiritual experience as vital to humanity and extolled contemporary writers and artists who promoted this truth in their creative work. Among those whom Buber especially valued was the German novelist Hermann Hesse, author of such spiritually oriented works as *Siddhartha, Steppenwolf, Journey to the East,* and *The Glass Bead Game.*

In July 1957, Buber offered an address entitled *Hermann Hesse's Service to the Spirit:*

> Asked to speak on the eightieth birthday of my friend Hermann Hesse, I felt and explained that I could not do what is expected at such an event: an evaluation of his total creative works. What I believed myself able to do and therefore under-

took is a pointing to the significance and the central section of these works, his series of great novels. . . .

Hermann Hesse has served the human spirit through the fact that he, as the storyteller that he is, has told of the contradiction between spirit and life, and of the conflict of the spirit against itself. In this way, he has made more visible the obstacle-ridden path that can lead to a new wholeness and unity. But as the man that he is, he has performed the same service through the fact that he always, where it was valid, has interceded for the wholeness and unity of the human being.

It is not the League of Eastern Wayfarers and the Bead Players alone who greet you today in all the world, Hermann Hesse. The servants of the spirit in all the world call out together a great greeting of love to you. Everywhere where one serves the spirit, you are loved.

Sigmund Freud and his friend Thomas Mann

Thomas Mann was a major German novelist whose most memorable works include *Death in Venice, The Magic Mountain*, and *Doctor Faustus*. He displayed a sharp intellect in his writings, focusing on cultural and political conditions of his time. He won the 1929 Nobel Prize for literature. Bitterly opposed to Nazism, Mann left Germany when Hitler came to power in 1933 and settled in Switzerland and the United States during his final decades.

Many prized Mann's novelistic wisdom and literary style of gentle irony. His friend Sigmund Freud sent this cynically tinged letter in June 1935:

Accept as a friend my affectionate greetings on your sixtieth birthday. I am one of your "oldest" readers and admirers, and I might wish you a very long and happy life as is the custom on such occasions. But I shall not do so. Wishing is cheap and strikes me as a relapse into the days when people believed in the magical omnipotence of thoughts. I think, too, from my most personal experience, that it is well if a compassionate fate sets a timely end to the length of our life.

Nor do I think the practice deserves imitation by which affection on these festive occasions [one] is compelled to hear himself loaded with praise as a man and analyzed and criticized as an artist. I shall not be guilty of such presumptions.

I can allow myself something else, however. In the name of a countless number of your contemporaries, I can express to you our confidence that you will never do or say—for an author's words are deeds—anything that is cowardly or base. Even in times and circumstances that perplex the judgment, you will take the right path and point it out to others.

Praising One's Mother

Louis Brandeis and his mother, Frederika

Serving as U.S. Supreme Court justice for nearly a quarter century until his retirement in 1939, Louis Brandeis was acclaimed for his legal precision and social vision; "the Brandeis brief" became a model for advocating the validity of social legislation. In our own era, Brandeis University, situated near Boston, was named after him.

The son of hardworking German-Jewish immigrants, Brandeis was still a young attorney in Boston when he wrote this short letter in November 1888 to his mother. He was already known as "the people's counsel" because of his many activities in the public interest:

> I must send you another birthday greeting and tell you how much I love you; that with each day I learn to extol your love and your worth more—and that when I look back over my life, I can find nothing in your treatment of me that I would alter. You often said, dearest mother, that I find fault; but I always told

you candidly that I felt and sought to change only after that little which appeared to me to be possible of improvement.

I believe, most beloved mother, that the improvement of the world—reform—can only arise when mothers like you are increased thousands of times and have more children.

Thomas Carlyle and his mother, Margaret

Scotsman Thomas Carlyle was a major social thinker in Victorian England. The eldest child of a stern, irascible stonemason, Carlyle showed intellectual precocity and attended the University of Edinburgh when he was fourteen. A widely read essayist and scholar, he addressed topics of personal heroism, democracy, and revolution.

In December 1844, Carlyle sent his mother this endearing letter:

Yesterday was my birthday. I meant to have written to you; I said to myself, "It is least thou canst do on *her* behalf for bringing thee into the world!" I rightfully purposed and meant; but just at the time intended for that pious object, an impertinent visitor was pleased to drop in, and my hands were tied! I reflect that you could not have got the letter any sooner at any rate, and so decided to write today.

Dear Mother, many thoughts, sure enough were in my head all yesterday! This time nine-and-forty years, I was small infant a few hours old, lying unconscious in your kind bosom; you piously rejoicing over me, appointing to love me while life lasted to us both. What a time to look back, through so many days, marked with all faithful labor by you, with joy and sorrow! ... Your poor "long sprawl of an ill-put-together thing" as you defined me, has grown up to be a distinct somewhat in this world, and his good mother's toil and travail with him was not entirely in vain....

I salute you for bringing me into the world, and for all your unwearied care over me there. God reward you for it, as assuredly He will and does. I never can reward you!

T. S. Eliot and his mother, Charlotte

The American poet T. S. Eliot is probably best known today for inspiring the long-running Broadway musical *Cats,* based on his 1939 work, *Old Possum's Book of Practical Cats.* However, Eliot was a first-rate poet whose earlier volumes included *The Love Song of J. Alfred Prufrock, The Four Quartets,* and *The Waste Land.* With his critical works and his poetry Eliot helped shape modern literature, the field for which he won a Nobel Prize in 1948. He also headed a publishing house for many years.

Eliot was born in St. Louis, but he settled in London as a young man; like his mentor Ezra Pound, he preferred the life of an expatriate to living in the United States. In November 1917, three years after moving to England, Eliot sent this letter to his mother:

I have your letter of October 22, and feel very sad at not having written on your birthday. I can hardly believe that you are seventy-four. No one would know it.

You are certainly the most wonderful woman of seventy-four that I have ever heard of, and I am very proud of you. I should be glad to think of having half your force and youth at that age.

You don't know how much satisfaction it has been through the last two years to think that I have parents whom I can be so convincingly proud of, who represent to me absolutely the best that America can produce; and by right of whom I feel that I can claim equality with anybody. Just to have ordinary, good commonplace parents would be inconceivably depressing—it would destroy one's confidence in all directions.

Theodore Roosevelt and his mother, Martha

Theodore Roosevelt was the youngest man ever to become U.S. President. He was forty-two when McKinley was assassinated in 1901. Roosevelt grew up frail and sickly with asthma, and suffered as a child his father's early death. He was devoted to his mother, and with her encouragement, he deliberately strengthened himself by vigorous exercise and sports. Later, as an admired Rough Rider and an influential political leader for a generation, he made the phrase "Speak softly and carry a big stick" famous and counseled his children to "Hit the line hard." Yet Roosevelt always valued loyalty and dependability more than physical prowess.

In July 1883, Roosevelt was vacationing in rural New York State when he happily wrote to his mother on her forty-eighth birthday:

> *Darling little Motherling,* Many, many happy returns, you sweetest little mother that ever lived! The pink wife and I have been talking of you and loving you ever so much, and wishing we could be with you today. And we were both saying how very much we had enjoyed your little visits to us last winter, and how pleased we were that you cared to come down to the little house. You must be down there just whenever you please all the time, as

often as you care to come, for the more often it is the warmer and warmer too your welcome would be.

This place is monotonous enough to give an angel the blues.

Richard Wagner and his mother, Johanna

Richard Wagner was a brilliant German composer who changed European musical, literary, and theatrical life. His most famous operas include *The Flying Dutchman, Tristan, The Valkyrie,* and *Tannhäuser.* Wagner taught that the theater should be the center of community culture, rather than merely a place for entertainment. During his life, he fought hard in the cause of artistic freedom and strongly influenced European culture with his music and ideas until World War I.

In September 1846, Wagner as a young man offered these words from Dresden for his mother's seventy-second birthday:

It is so long since I congratulated you upon your birthday, that it does me real good to be able to observe the proper day at last— so often overlooked by me, alas, in the hurry of business—to tell you how profoundly it rejoices me to know you're nearer us yet in soul and body, be able still to squeeze your hand from time to time, and recall together with and through yourself my youth you once cherished and shielded. Only in the realization that you abide with us yet, can your children still distinctly feel themselves one family. Whom life has blown hither and thither, to knit fresh bonds of kindred here and there, when they think of you, their dear old Mother, who has formed no other ties upon this earth than those which knit her to her children, they all are one again, thy bairns!

May God preserve you long in full possession of your faculties, that to your life's end you may reap the only joy you can upon this earth: the joy of a sympathetic onlooker at your children's prosperity!

Proclaiming Admiration to a Statesman

Julio S. and his inspiration, John F. Kennedy

John F. Kennedy was very much enamored of his two children, Caroline and John Jr. In January 1961, when the forty-three-year-old Kennedy took office as president, his daughter was a toddler and his son newly born. Later, President Theodore Roosevelt's daughter Alice Roosevelt Longworth was visiting the Kennedys at the White House and observed how casually the children ran around the family's living quarters on the second floor. She remarked, "This is just the way it was when I lived here."

During his brief term in office, the glamorous young president received thousands of letters and postcards from youngsters throughout the United States. Some offered political or policy-making advice on topics ranging from the cold war, to space exploration and public education—but most were simply adoring. In his entertaining book,

Kids' Letters to President Kennedy, author Bill Adler included the following, affectionate letter in 1961 from Julio S:

I received the picture that you sent me and like it very much. Someday I may be able to come to the White House.

The closest I have ever gotten to it was on July 28th—my birthday—when I went over to the [White House] gates. There I saw Caroline's ducks. I bet she has a lot of fun with them. But my favorite things are cars and trucks.

By the way, we will be moving to Chicago in a few weeks. When we move, I will write to you and tell you what it is like. Well, it is dark and after my bedtime so I think I'll say goodbye.

Promising Courage to One's Father

❦

Ulysses S. Grant and his father, Jesse Grant

Grant, the eighteenth president of the United States, is best remembered for his prowess in leading the Union Army to victory over Lee's southern force and decisively ending the Civil War. Later, at the end of Grant's life, he wrote his *Memoirs,* published posthumously in 1885. The work became a huge bestseller and brought his widow considerable wealth.

A day before his fortieth birthday, in April 1862, Grant was directing his troops camped by Pittsburg Landing, Tenneessee. There he penned these confident words to his elderly father, Jesse, a wealthy tanner:

> I will go on, and do my duty to the very best of my ability, without praise, and do all I can to bring this war to a speedy close. I am not an aspirant for anything at the close of the war.

There is one thing I feel well assured of: that is, that I have the confidence of every brave man in my command. Those who showed the white feather will do all in their power to attract attention from themselves. I had perhaps a dozen officers arrested for cowardice in the first day's fight at this place. These men are necessarily my enemies.

As to the talk about a surprise here, nothing could be more false. If the enemy had sent us word when and where they should attack us, we could not have been better prepared. Skirmishing had been going on for two days between our reconnoitering parties and the enemy's advance. I did not believe, however, that they intended to make a determined attack, but simply that they were making a reconnaisance in force.

Reflecting on the Day's Events

Dorothy Wordsworth

William Wordsworth is among the most admired English Romantic poets. In his long life, he wrote more than five hundred sonnets. In 1843 he was appointed his nation's poet laureate. Wordsworth's celebrated masterpiece was his long autobiographical poem "The Prelude: Growth of a Poet's Mind." Orphaned as children, he and his younger sister Dorothy—less than eighteen months his junior—grew to be extremely close. They traveled widely as companions, and they kept a rural house together for seven years, until William was married in 1802. During this period, they shared an inspirational friendship with the poet Samuel Taylor Coleridge, who lived nearby.

In the early hours of Christmas Day (her birthday) 1802, Dorothy Wordsworth offered these ruminations in her journal:

My beloved William is turning over the leaves of Charlotte Smith's sonnets, but he keeps his hand to his poor chest, pushing aside his breastplate. Mary is well and I am well, and Molly is blithe as last year at this time. Coleridge came this morning with Wedgwood. We all turned out of William's bedroom one by one to meet him. He looked well. We had to tell him of the birth of his little girl, born yesterday morning at 6 o'clock.

It was not an unpleasant morning to the feeling! Far from it. The sun shone now and then, and there was no wind, but all things looked cheerless and distinct: no meltings of sky into mountains, the mountains like stone wrought up with huge hammers.

I am thirty-one years of age. It is a dull, frosty day.

Relating Confidence to One's Mother

❧

Robert Edwin Peary and his mother, Josephine

Robert Edwin Peary was one of the great Arctic explorers. He was raised in rural Pennsylania and attended Bowdoin College and embarked on a career as a draftsman for the U.S. Coastal and Geodetic Survey, then became a civil engineer for the U.S. Navy. Starting in 1886 with a trip into the interior of Greenland, Peary became an increasingly important—and famous—figure in Arctic explorations. Historians today debate whether Peary actually reached the North Pole in 1909 as he claimed, but there's no doubt about his life of achievement.

Peary's father died when the lad was only three years old, and he grew up close to his devoted mother, Josephine. On his twentieth birthday, in May 1876, Peary shared these inspiring thoughts with her:

> The only way I have celebrated is by indulging in vague wonderings: whether [my] contest with the world will be harder than

[my] contest with college? Will it prove too much for me? Whether in ten years I shall be in Maine, in Patagonia, in Sweden or in Australia, or whether it will all be blank to me then.

It seems almost an impossibility to me how anyone, as some of our farmers do, can look forward to living their life out in the same place and doing the same things that their fathers and grandfathers did before them. Today, as I think of what the world is, and that I have my life before me, nothing seems impossible.

I wish that as in the story books, some fairy might place the mirror of my life before me and tell me to look at whatever scene I wished. Yet, if it could be so, I can hardly say but I should close my eyes and refuse to look. How many have wished and wondered about the mysterious future as I do. And yet, if the curtain were permitted to be drawn aside, would shrink from doing it, for fear of gazing upon rugged rocks and yawning graves, in place of the velvety paths they wish for.

Reminiscing About Youthful Achievement

Alec Guinness

The English actor Alec Guinness is best remembered today for his role as Luke Skywalker's uncle and Jedi mentor Obiwan Kanobe, in the immensely popular *Star Wars* film series. Among Guinness's most famous movies are *The Bridge on the River Kwai, Brother Sun, Sister Moon,* and *A Passage to India.* On stage, his highly regarded performances include Hamlet and Macbeth. He was knighted in 1959 for his accomplishments in theater and film.

In Guinness's intriguing memoir, *My Name Escapes Me,* the renowned actor offered this diary entry on his eighty-second birthday, in April 1996:

> Sixty-two years ago today I made my first professional appearance, at the King's Theater, Hammersmith—long demolished. The play was *Libel!* Put on, directed and acted in by Leon M. Lion,

a rather alarming, taciturn, beetle-browed actor/manager. . . . My humble job was to sit in the jury box wearing a lot of make-up. I think I was paid twelve shillings for the week we were there, but this was raised to a pound when we moved to the Playhouse. There was an extremely kind stage-manager, Matthew Forsyth, who gave me two lines to understudy.

When I got home this afternoon, I found a vast pile of [birthday] mail which dismayed me, knowing I shall have to write thank-you notes for much of it. Matthew had come down yesterday and kindly left me his usual plethora of brilliantly chosen gadgets. This year he provided me with something which recharges ordinary batteries, a Japanese contraption which enhances sound and a "miracle" watering-can which directs a jet of water wherever you want it to go. That is going to be very useful as Merula has given me a trough of beautiful, variegated hydrangeas.

Revealing Love to One's Son

Lydia Jackson Emerson and her son Edward

Lydia Jackson Emerson, the second wife of Ralph Waldo Emerson, America's leading nineteenth-century philosopher, was well known for her wit and eloquence. Born in Plymouth, Massachussetts, she and her two siblings were raised by relatives after their mother died in early life from tuberculosis. With a highly disciplined mind, Lydia was admirably self-taught, and together with eight women friends in Plymouth, she organized a Reading Society and issued a newsletter called *The Wisdom of the Nine.*

She and Ralph Waldo Emerson married in 1835, four years after his first wife's death, and the year before his first book, *Nature,* was published to wide acclaim. From the outset, their mutual attraction was intense. Lydia shared her husband's mystical, poetic outlook on life, and became close with several of his friends, including Henry

David Thoreau. She was a devoted mother. As her four children entered their teenage years, Lydia's admonition was always common sense: "Our confidence in you is entire, and there is no need to give you minute directions."

In July 1863 Lydia penned this affectionate letter to her son Edward on his nineteenth birthday:

> It may have seemed to you that your mother thought but lightly of your birthday yesterday, by her apparent levity in speaking of it. But in my usual night watch, I realized with joy and gratitude the greatness of the gift which God in indulgent kindness had given us. . . .
>
> After the door closed upon you, mutual congratulations passed between your father and mother, that we are blessed with such a son. But we do this *oftener* than once a year. The mercy that has brought you safely through so many dangers and trials, we joyfully appreciate.
>
> If you would surely keep your life true and good, and happy to the end, do not renounce [religious] study. Regularly read from Scripture until you learn to value the blessed book, for then faith, hope, and aspiration will not fade from your soul in the struggle of life.

Revealing Playfulness to a Friend

———

Albert Einstein and his friend Samuel Gronemann

It's both ironic and meaningful that Albert Einstein, the genius who transformed human understanding of space and time, was typically playful in response to celebrations of his birthday. For example, when he turned fifty in March 1929, Einstein fled his Berlin apartment and went into hiding for privacy. When the event was over, he solved the problem of having to thank his worldwide friends for their birthday gifts and messages by composing a humorous poem and mailing printed copies inscribed with a brief, personal greeting to each.

Among Einstein's long-time friends was the multifaceted Samuel Gronemann: a Berlin lawyer, author, playwright, and Jewish leader who fled Nazi Germany to help found the State of Israel. In *Albert Einstein: The Human Side,* Helen Dukas and Banesh Hoffmann related that, in March 1949, for Einstein's seventieth birthday in

Princeton, Gronemann sent a poetic letter from Tel Aviv containing these (translated) verses:

> One who, after struggling many a night,
> Can't get Relativity quite right;
> Yes, one who has no feeling of alarm,
> Because coordinates never did him harm,
> He argues thus, and does so most politely;
> If seventy-year-old Einstein still feels sprightly,
> Then one can irrefutably deduce
> That Einstein's theory has a practical use.
> With friendly throngs surrounding you to pay
> Homage on your seventieth natal day,
> I, too, will show no doubts or hesitations
> In offering us and you congratulations.
> For we in Israel, as you'll understand,
> Think of you as ours in this land.

Einstein replied promptly with this jovial response:

> Non-comprehenders are often distressed.
> Not you, though, because with good humor you're blessed.
> After all, your thoughts went like this, I dare say:
> It was none but the Lord who made us that way.

The Lord takes revenge—and it's simply unfair.
For he himself made the weakness we bear.
And lacking defense we succumb to this badness,
Sometimes in triumph, and sometimes in sadness.

But rather than stubbornly uttering curses,
You bring us salvation by means of your verses,
Which are cunningly made so the just and the sinners
End by counting themselves all as winners.

Revealing Sadness to a Friend

⚬━⚬━⚬━

Dylan Thomas and his friend Vernon Watkins

"I hold a beast, an angel, and a madman inside of me," declared Dylan Thomas, one of Britain's leading mid-twentieth century poets. Born in Swansea, Wales, Thomas worked briefly as a journalist before embarking on a freelance literary career. Despite a short life marked by alcoholism and depression, Thomas achieved lasting fame for such prose works as *Adventures in the Skin Trade, Portrait of the Artist as a Young Dog*, and *Quite Early One Morning.* He also published many short stories, wrote film scripts, broadcast stories and talks, and wrote *Under Milkwood,* a radio play for voices.

In October 1938, upon the occasion of his birthday, he sent his friend Vernon Watkins this rather gloomy poem. Thomas's recent marriage at the time seemed to have done little to raise his spirits; the following year, he published it in *The Map of Love.*

BIRTHDAY POEM

Twenty-four years remind the tears of my eyes.
(Bury the dead for fear that they walk to the grave in labour).
In the groin of the natural doorway I crouched like a tailor
Sewing a shroud for a journey
By the light of the meat-eating sun.
Dressed to die, the sensual strut begun,
With my red veins full of money,
In the final direction of the elementary town
I advance for as long as forever is.

Next to the poem Thomas scribbled to his friend, "This poem's just a statement perhaps. It's for my birthday, just arriving. I'm pleased, terribly, with this—so far. Do tell me, and type please."

The Secret of Reaching a Hundred

Grandma Moses (Anna Mary Robertson)

"If I didn't start painting, I would have raised chickens," quipped Anna Mary Robertson, a crusty, feisty, upstate New York farmwoman and grandmother who gained fame in the mid-twentieth century for her primitive artistry begun in old age.

After raising ten children and working hard at a variety of jobs, Anna devoted herself full-time to art in the 1930s, when she began exhibiting her work—mostly of placid rural life—in county fairs. "Discovered" in the window of a Hoosick Falls, New York, drugstore by a Manhattan art collector in 1938, Anna's paintings were soon placed on exhibit in the Museum of Modern Art, and eventually featured in leading art galleries and publications. Anna became a celebrity over the next two decades, and on September 7, 1960, New York State governor Nelson Rockefeller proclaimed the date as Grandma Moses Day, in celebration of her one hundredth birthday.

President Dwight Eisenhower and his wife, Mamie, sent a congratulatory letter from the White House, and former President Harry Truman and his wife, Bess, sent a similar tribute from Independence, Missouri. The post office of Eagle Bridge, New York, was almost buried beneath an avalanche of birthday cards, letters, and gifts from all over the United States.

Moses had protested the celebration of her one hundredth birthday, but outnumbered by well-wishers, she finally relented. As throngs of admirers streamed through her house, she said cheerfully: "I'm going to sit right here, just so, and the others can do the work. I wish they wouldn't fuss, but it's a nice excuse for the young people to get together." Then, fulfilling a promise made to herself some weeks before the event, Moses danced a jig with her reluctant, eighty-four-year-old physician.

To protect Moses from stress, her family restricted the number of reporters permitted to interview her. Among the fortunate ones was Joy Miller of the Associated Press, whose article was printed in newspapers across the country:

> Your impression of Grandma Moses is that she's very fragile and very old. She's sitting in the livingroom, looking small at one end of a big sofa. . . . Her welcoming hand grasps yours with startling vigor. As she chats about this and that, the character of

a remarkable woman emerges—kindly, humorous, unaffected, indomitable, with sight and hearing in admirable repair. You become aware that her seemingly frail 100-pound frame supports a spirit that's at once robust and ageless.

When asked by reporters on how to live to be a hundred, Grandma Moses readily offered this advice: "Laugh a lot. Tell jokes. If you are alone, think of jokes. Keep happy. Keep busy. That's how to do it."

Seeking One's Roots

⌇⌇⌇⌇

Bob Dylan

More than just a highly popular songwriter and concert performer, in his youth Bob Dylan became a symbol for this entire generation. In the tumultuous years of the 1960s, his impassioned songs like "Blowin' in the Wind" and "The Times, They Are A-Changin" were indelibly associated with social causes like civil rights, antiwar rallies, and candlelit marches. They gained him the stature of a cultural icon.

To the sixties generation, whose slogan was "Never trust anyone over thirty," one's thirtieth birthday carried a lot of significance back then. In May 1971, Bob Dylan celebrated his thirtieth birthday in Jerusalem with his wife, Sara Lowndes. He made a visit to the Western Wall of the Holy Temple in the Old City, where, ironically, he was accidentally photographed by a UPI photographer. When the photographer realized that he had captured Bob Dylan, né Robert Zimmerman, in the homeland of his ancestors on his thirtieth birthday, the photo was widely syndicated around the world and rumors flew that Dylan was embracing the religion of his forebears.

Later that evening, he and Sara went to see a Gregory Peck movie. Dylan's subsequent ballad *Brownsville Girl* celebrated the venerable actor's ability—especially in the cowboy-Western *The Gunslinger*—and contained the convincing lyric, "I'd see him in anything."

Sharing Childhood Nostalgia With a Friend

—◦—◦—

Ben Washam and his friend Chuck Jones

Chuck Jones was a Warner Brothers animator who helped create such memorable cartoon characters as Bugs Bunny, Daffy Duck, Elmer Fudd, and Wile E. Coyote. "We were grossly underpaid," Jones recalled about his work team, "but we were being paid to do what we enjoyed doing. We were being paid to associate every day with people we loved and respected, people who were eager, excited and joyfully willing to try almost anything." On the occasion of Jones's sixty-fifth birthday, in September 1981, his friend and fellow Warner Brothers animator Ben Washam offered this affectionate reminiscence:

> On my tenth birthday, my father gave me a mule. It was truly love at first sight. I named him Spencer after a rifle I saw advertised in a Sears Roebuck catalog. The spring and summer that

followed were the most wonderful in my memory. We rode over and through every hill and swamp in northeast Arkansas.

In the fall after the crops were in, everybody went to the country fair, especially Spencer and me. Aside from judging cows, pigs, chickens, cakes, pies, and the like, stump-pulling was a community favorite.

The stumps were dynamited out of the ground a few days before the fair started, then a mule was hitched to the stump. The mule that pulled the greatest distance won. Well, Spencer and me won.

First prize was a Rhode Island Red Rooster and a blue ribbon with Robert E. Lee's face painted on it with gold paint. I was so proud I kissed Spencer. Everybody laughed and my mother made me wash my face. Everything was fine, I even got a piece of cake. The soda pop was great, and I saved half of it for Spencer. . . . My reason for telling you this is to wish you happy birthday.

Sharing Exciting News With a Friend

❧

Robert Frost and his friend Louis Untermeyer

Robert Frost was among America's greatest modern poets. To paraphrase one of his own lines of verse, he repeatedly "took the road less traveled by." To the chagrin of his grandfather, Frost dropped out of first Dartmouth and then Harvard to become a farmer-poet in rural New Hampshire. The hours on the thirty-acre farm near Derry were long, but Robert and his wife, Elinor, led a simple existence raising four children (a fifth died from illness).

In March 1950, Senator Robert Taft introduced the following United States Senate resolution in honor of Frost's seventy-fifth birthday (it was unanimously accepted):

> Whereas Robert Frost in his books of poetry has given the American people a long series of stories and lyrics which are

enjoyed, repeated, and thought about by people of all ages and callings; and

Whereas these poems have helped to guide American thought, humor and wisdom, setting forth to our minds a reliable representation of ourselves and of all men; and

Whereas his work throughout the past half century has enhanced for many their understanding of the United States and their love of country; and

Whereas on March 26th he will celebrate his seventy-fifth birthday:

Therefore be it

Resolved, That the Senate of the United States extend him felicitations of the Nation which he has served so well.

A few weeks later, Frost sent his friend, poet Louis Untermeyer, a copy of the U.S. Senate Resolution honoring him and humorously added this terse sentence: "My only comment is the senatorial 'No comment.'"

Sharing Humor With Friends

John F. Kennedy and his friend Marilyn Monroe

John F. Kennedy was the youngest person ever elected president, and he was the youngest to die in office. Despite Kennedy's short time in the Oval Office—less than three years—he carved out for himself through his charismatic personality a unique place in American culture and history. A youthful, handsome president, he exuded vim and vigor. Kennedy's most famous public birthday occurred in May 1962.

In *John F. Kennedy and Marilyn Monroe,* biographers Judie Mills and Donald Spoto recounted that:

JFK got more good news just before his forty-fifth birthday, when on May 24th, Lieutenant Scott Carpenter became the second American to orbit the earth. The President had also enjoyed an early birthday celebration at a Democratic fund-raising event in Madison Square Garden. Two chefs bore a huge cake aloft; the climactic moment of that evening came when Marilyn Monroe, with whom Kennedy was rumored to have had an affair, appeared onstage. Attired in what she called "skin and beads" the movie actress gave a slightly off-key but steamy rendition of "Happy Birthday, Mr. President."

Halfway into his twenty-minute address, Kennedy thanked the performers individually, commenting that, "Miss Monroe left a picture to come all the way East, and I can now retire from politics after having had 'Happy Birthday' sung to me in such a sweet, wholesome way." It was but one of many laugh lines that combined political rhetoric, wit, good cheer, and earnest allusions to important social issues.

Sharing Joyful News With One's Mother

William Randolph Hearst and his mother, Phoebe

For more than a half century, William Randolph Hearst Sr. exerted a tremendous influence on American journalism and politics. As a public figure, he was larger than life—first as an ambitious congressman, then as a reclusive yet active businessman, living in the famous castle that rises above the Pacific Ocean at San Simeon. Creator of a media empire, Hearst enjoyed a lifestyle of immense wealth and privilege. But perhaps because he had been born into money, Hearst always wanted his five children to be successful in their own right. After his first three sons were born, Hearst's wife, Millicent, gave birth to twin boys on December 2, 1915.

The following day, William sent his mother this jesting telegram:

George, William, John and also Elbert and Edward—or whatever their names will be—hope you had a happy birthday and wish you would come as soon as possible to New York. Millicent and I second these sentiments. The twins must have excellent consciences, judging from the way they sleep. Furthermore, they both have blue eyes, florid complexions and fine tenor voices.

Sharing News About Travel

Rupert Brooke and his friend Cathleen Norris

The gifted young English poet Rupert Brooke was among the millions of young men who lost their lives fighting in World War I. In August 1913, some two years before his death, Brooke was vacationing with friends abroad when he sent this happy letter to his beloved, Cathleen Norris:

> Today, o my heart, I am twenty-six years old. And I've done so little. I'm very much ashamed. By God, I'm going to make things hum, though.
>
> But that's all so far away. I'm lying quite naked on a beach of golden sand, six miles from the hunting-lodge, the other man near by, a gun between us in case bears appear, the boat pulled up on the shore, the lake very blue and ripply, and the sun rather strong.

We bathed off the beach, and then lit a fire of birch and spruce, and fried eggs and ate cold caribou-heart, and made tea, and had (oh!) blueberry pie. Cooking and eating a meal naked is the most solemnly primitive thing one can do.

And so, you must realize that I'm living far the most wonderfully, and incredibly romantic life you've ever heard of, and *infinitely* superior to your miserable crawling London existence.

Lord Bryon and his friend John Murray

Lord Byron was among the most colorful of Romantic poets. He lived an adventurous life that, for nearly two centuries, many have found as evocative as his verse. He valued fellow poet Percy Shelley among his closest friends and enjoyed many romantic liaisons. Traveling widely, Byron set many of his poems in Europe and the Near East, based on his personal experiences in Greece, Portugal, Spain, and Albania. Byron's major works include *Hours of Idleness, The Bride of Abydos,* and his unfinished epic, *Don Juan.*

Arriving in the south Scottish village of Newstead with his half sister, Augusta Leigh, in mid-January 1814, Bryon wrote this self-congratulatory letter on his birthday to his friend John Murray:

You will be glad to hear of my safe arrival here. The time of my return will depend upon the weather, which is so impracticable that this [communication] has to advance through more snows than ever opposed the Emperor [Napoleon]'s retreat. The roads are impassible—and return impossible—for the present, which I do not regret, as I am at my ease and six and twenty completes this day: a very pretty age if it would always last.

Our coals are excellent, our fireplaces large, my cellar full, and my head empty—and I have not yet recovered my joy at leaving London. If any unexpected turn occurred with my purchaser, I believe I should hardly quit the place at all, but shut my doors and let my beard grow.

Ezra Pound and his mother, Isabel

Ezra Pound is ranked among the twentieth century's greatest poets. *The Cantos,* composed over fifty years but never completed, is considered his most important work. Over a long career, Pound encouraged and influenced such luminaries as T. S. Eliot, Robert Frost, and Ernest Hemingway at the start of their literary careers. His friends included the Irish writers James Joyce and William Butler Yeats.

Disillusioned by what he considered the artistic backwardness of the United States, Pound landed in Gibraltar in 1907 and remained an expatriate in Europe for most of his life. After broadcasting profascist commentaries in Italy during World War II, Pound was arrested by U.S. forces, tried for treason, and committed to a mental hospital in Washington, D.C.

In November 1913, Pound was twenty-eight years old and visiting in London when he wrote his mother:

I plan to spend my birthday largesse in the purchase of four luxurious undershirts. Or rather I had planned to do so; if, however, the bloody guardsman who borrowed my luxurious hat from the Cabaret cloak room (not by accident) does not return the same, I shall probably divert certain shekels up on the yeager.

My stay in Stone Cottage will not be in the least profitable. I detest the country. Yeats will amuse part of the time and bore me to death with psychical research the rest. I regard the visit as a duty to posterity . . . I seem to spend most of my time attending to other peoples' affairs, weaning young poetettes from obscurity into the glowing pages of divers rotten publications or conducting a literary kindergarten for the aspiring. . . .

Anyhow, it is settled that you come over in the Spring. If dad can't come then, we'll try to arrange that for the year after.... You will come over in April; at least, you will plan to be here for May and June. Once here, you can hang out at Dutchess Street quite as cheaply as you could at home.

I shall go to a Welsh lake later in the season instead of going to Garda in the Spring. Having been in the country through the winter, I shall probably not need spring cleaning.

Sharing a Quiet Party With One's Family

Harpo Marx

Next to his younger brother Groucho, Harpo was undoubtedly the best known of the Marx Brothers. His comedic character was a frenzied, mischievous mute who played the harp and communicated by honking a horn. Harpo starred in such celebrated films as *Duck Soup, Horse Feathers, A Night at the Opera,* and *A Day at the Races.* After the Marx Brothers broke up, Harpo was never so popular, but perhaps that didn't matter as much to him as it did to others. As his favorite brother, Groucho, once quipped, "He inherited all my mother's good qualities—kindness, understanding, and friendliness. I got what was left."

In his autobiography, *Harpo Speaks!* the comic actor offered this reminiscence:

I felt a little pang when I turned fifty-six. My father, Aleck, had just turned fifty-six when he died. Susan and the kids didn't let me mope very long over my age. They turned on the Christmas lights in honor of my birthday, and the pang went away. It was nowhere near Christmas, and the lights were hung in a jacaranda tree in the patio, but this was our joint and this was the way we ran it.

One Christmas, the kids had been so enchanted by the jacarandas strung by colored lights that we didn't have the heart to take them down. So we left them connected in the tree, and turned them on whenever we felt like declaring a holiday. The lights were turned on for all of our birthdays.

Sharing Teenage Fun With One's Brother

A. A. Milne and his brother, Kenneth

The famed author of *Winnie the Pooh, Now We Are Six,* and *The House at Pooh Corner* grew up in late Victorian London. While studying at Cambridge, he edited the undergraduate magazine *Granta,* later joined the staff of *Punch* as an assistant editor, and became well known for his light essays and comedies. In recent years, the *Pooh* series has enjoyed an incredible resurgence of appeal and even spurred the publication of several business management books based on its purported insights about motivation and leadership.

Milne was especially close to his brother Ken, sixteen months older, and in middle age he dedicated his *Autobiography* "to the memory of Kenneth John Milne, who bore the worst of me and made the best of me." In this work, A. A. Milne recounted how, as teenagers, they avidly enjoyed composing humorous poetry together:

Writing light verse in collaboration is easier than one would think, for a set of light verses, like a scene of stage dialogue, is never finished. One can go on and on, searching for the better word, the more natural phrase. There comes a time when one is in danger of losing all sense of values, and then one's collaborator steps in suddenly with what one sees at once is the perfect word.

On January 18th, I was eighteen. Ken sent me a pocket-size book, and (since we were in that vein) a charming set of laudatory verses. I wish I could print them here, as a tribute not to myself but to him. Like many other things which I wish that I had kept, they are gone, even from my memory. I went back to school, almost for the first time, happy.

Taking a Getaway With One's Daughter

◆━◆━◆━◆

Erica Jong and her daughter, Molly

Though she is the author of seventeen works of fiction, essays, and poetry, Erica Jong is still undoubtedly best known for her novel *Fear of Flying,* published in 1973. For many at the time, it personified a new feminism celebrating sensuality and bodily pleasure. A lifelong New Yorker, Jong continues to address such themes in her writing. In her humorous but evocative memoir, *Fear of Fifty,* she declared at the outset:

> At fifty, the last thing I wanted was a public celebration. Three days before my birthday, I took off for a spa in the Berkshires with my daughter, Molly (then thirteen), slept in the same bed with her, giggling before sleep, slumber party style, worked out all day (as if I were a jock, not a couch potato), learned trendy low-fat vegetarian recipes, had my blackheads expunged,

my flab massaged, my muscles stretched, and thought about the second half of my life.

These thoughts alternated between terror and acceptance. Turning fifty, I thought, is like flying: hours of boredom punctuated by moments of sheer terror. . . .

What was happening to me in the second part of my life? I was getting myself back and I liked that self. I was getting the humor, the intensity, the balance I had known in childhood. But I was getting it back with a dividend. Call it serenity. Call it wisdom. I knew what mattered and what did not. . . .

Is fifty too young to start an autobiography? Of course, it is. But maybe eighty is too old. . . .

Fifty is the time when time itself begins to seem short. The sense of time running out has been exacerbated by the AIDS epidemic and the deaths of so many friends still in their thirties, forties, and fifties. Who knows whether there will be a better time? The time is always now.

I write this book from a place of self-acceptance, cleansing, anger, and raucous laughter.

I am old enough to know that laughter, not anger, is the true revelation.

Teaching A Child About Goals

~·~·~·~

C. S. Lewis and his goddaughter Sarah

The Oxford scholar and writer C. S. Lewis was acclaimed for his fantasy novels like *The Chronicles of Narnia* and popular religious essays. He never had any children of his own, but he was a devoted godfather. And after becoming famous as a religious writer in the post-World War II era, Lewis maintained an active, fatherly correspondence with youngsters who wrote to him from all over the world.

As recorded in *C. S. Lewis, Letters to Children,* edited by Lyle Dorsett and Marjorie Mead, the famous writer in April 1949 offered these wry congratulatory words to his goddaughter Sarah:

> I am sorry to say that I don't think I shall be able to be at your confirmation on Saturday. For most men Saturday afternoon is a free time, but I have an invalid old lady to look after and the weekend is the time when I have no freedom at all, and have to

be Nurse, Kennel-Maid, Wood-Cutter, Butler, House-Maid, and Secretary all in one.

If I *had* come and we had met, I am afraid you might have found me very shy and dull. (By the way, always remember that old people can be quite as shy with young people as young people can be with old. This explains what must seem to you the idiotic way in which so many grown-ups talk to you.)

[As this is your confirmation], I have one [useful] piece of advice. Remember that there are only three kinds of things anyone need ever do. (1) Things we *ought* to do. (2) Things we've *got* to do. (3) Things we *like* doing. I say this because some people seem to spend so much of their time doing things for none of the three reasons, things like reading books they don't like because other people read them.

Things you ought to do are things like doing your homework and being nice to people. Things one has got to do are things like dressing and undressing, or household shopping. Things one likes doing—but of course, I don't know what *you* like. Perhaps you'll write and tell me one day.

Of course, I always mention you in my prayers and will most especially on Saturday. Do the same for me.

Teaching Resourcefulness

✦✦✦✦✦

Dorotea Chavez and her son Cesar

Cesar Chavez was the charismatic founder and leader of the United Farm Workers of America. Establishing this organization in 1962 to improve the conditions of migrant laborers, Chavez made an impression on the American consciousness. To better the lives of these migrant workers, he organized successful boycotts of produce such as lettuce and grapes. Largely due to his efforts, the UFWA won its first contracts in 1970.

Raised in rural Arizona by Mexican immigrants, Chavez knew poverty from first-hand experience. His family became migrant farm workers during the Great Depression; while growing up, he and his siblings attended more than thirty public schools. In his memoir *Cesar Chavez: Autobiography of La Causa,* the influential labor organizer recalled his first move westward, in 1939 into California:

We arrived in San Jose on June 24, my mother's birthday, and stopped on Jackson Street by an isolated barrio where many farm workers lived. Again, we had no place to stay.

The barrio wasn't large, just two unpaved dead-end streets running into Jackson and bordered on three sides by fields and pasture. It was no different than poor barrios are today.... shabby shacks and old houses with outside privies in the back. There were, of course, no sewers. Each lot was crowded with several houses and surrounded by tall, unpainted fences. In those two long blocks ther were also maybe six Pentecostal churches. And there were lots of people.

This was the barrio called *Sal Si Puedes*—Get Out if You Can—and it is still prominent today, probably because it's dirtier and uglier than the others.... But when we arrived [there], our problem was getting in, not out.... My mother asked the ladies whether there was a house where we could stay that night. Our two cars, loaded with mattresses, baggage, and kids, told every-one a familiar story. But the answer was always the same. They were too crowded. There was no room.

Finally, one lady told her of an old man who might have a room. "But he's crazy," she said.

"He's not very well, Don Pedro," someone else warned.

"We'll chance it," said my mother. "See what happens. I have to put my children somewhere tonight. . . ."

We were told nobody liked Pedro in the barrio. He was supposed to be a mean, tough guy who didn't like children and chased them out of his yard. He had fruit trees, and when they tried to steal the fruit, he would hit them.

But when my mother, who could make friends with anybody, talked to him, Don Pedro agreed to let us have a room which he had rented to a Chilean schoolteacher named Manuel. Although the Chilean got very angry at having to move, Don Pedro insisted.

"This family can't stay in the street, Manuel. You move out of this room and use the little room. They're going to take this room," he said.

As it turned out, he was a good man, just a little eccentric. He thought we were well-mannered, which, at first, surprised him. So he even got to like us.

Teaching Values to One's Children

Dr. Edward Hemingway and his son Ernest

As one of America's greatest novelists, Ernest Hemingway produced such twentieth-century classics as *A Farewell to Arms, The Sun Also Rises*, and *For Whom the Bell Tolls*. While working as a journalist for the *Kansas City Star* before serving as a Red Cross volunteer in Italy during World War I, Hemingway developed the plain, forceful writing style that became his hallmark.

Hemingway grew up in an affluent family in Oak Park, Illinois. By adolescence, he showed a wild streak that especially upset his father, a hardworking physician. As recounted by Michael Reynolds in *The Young Hemingway,* for his twenty-first birthday in July 1922, Ernest's mother prepared a lavish feast for him and a chum, Ted Brumback. But his disapproving father sent only a five-dollar check for a present. Irritated by the stingy gift, Ernest refused to cash it—whereupon Edward Hemingway fired off this sobering birthday letter:

Try not to be a sponger. It is best for you and Ted to change camps and go to new fields to conquer. It is altogether too hard on your mother to entertain you and your friends when she is not having help and you are so hard to please and so insulting to your dear mother.

So please pack up and try elsewhere until you are again invited to [stay with us at] Windemere. Try and look this matter square in the face as an honest boy, and be as kind and considerate to your mother and sisters [as you are to your friends' families].

Sam Houston and his son Sam Houston Jr.

The greatest name in Texas is still that of Sam Houston: military commander, creator of the Lone Star State, influential congressman, and then senator of the new state of Texas until it seceded from the Union in 1861. During that period, in February 1859, Sam Houston offered this surprising advice to his son, Sam Houston Jr., upon his sixteenth birthday:

In writing you in my last letter, I did not admonish you not to carry concealed weapons.

I hope that you will never do it, and were I with you I could state my reasons, which I am sure you would approve, with your perceptions of propriety. And oh, my son, by all means keep from the use of tobacco. Don't smoke or chew. Besides the habit of its use it is an expense and trouble. I look to you as one on whom my mantle is to fall, and I wish to leave it to you, without a rent in it. It is natural that I should desire you to wear it worthily, aye nobly, and to give additional lustre to all that may descend to you! If you have a suitable opportunity, I wish you to pay more attention to Language, History, Geography, and Grammar, than to Mathematics. If this can be done delicately, I wish it done, not otherwise. . . .

Thomas Huxley and his son Leonard

Thomas Huxley was an influential nineteenth-century English scientist and advocate of Darwin's theory of evolution. His elder son, Leonard, became an educator and editor of the *Cornhill Magazine,* and authored books on biography and poetry. In 1881 Thomas Huxley sent Leonard this letter on his twenty-first birthday:

> You will have a son some day yourself, I suppose, and if you do, I can wish you no greater satisfaction than to be able to say that he has reached manhood without ever having given you a

serious anxiety, and that you can look forward with entire confidence to his playing the man in the battle of life.

I have tried to make you feel your responsibilities and act independently as early as possible. But, once for all, remember, that I am not only your father, but your nearest friend, ready to help you in all things reasonable, and perhaps in a few unreasonable. . . .

Lincoln Steffens and his son, Peter

A crusading journalist, Lincoln Steffens became famous at the turn of the twentieth century as a muckraker seeking major reforms in American society. He helped arouse the nation's social conscience by exposing the greed, corruption, and sordid dealings of politicians and "captains of industry" in countless newspapers and magazine articles.

In a letter of November 1933, Steffens offered this vivid advice—on the importance of teamwork—to his son, Peter:

> You have had your ninth birthday. Turned the critical age of nine. Do you feel the difference? You must. There are a lot of your kid tastes that you should pass. No more stealing, no more lying; better table and other manners. For you have to clear the deck for ten. You will, of course. I am not a bit worried.

I went to the Harvard-Yale football game yesterday. Harvard won by 19–6, and rejoiced because for two or three years Yale has always won. It was team-work that did it, team-work, discipline and skill. One big play was a long straight pass; one man passed to a second man who ran up to where it was prearranged that the ball was to go. Perfect. Another fine play is described by the papers as a nine-yard run, but I saw it and the point I noted was that the Harvard team, the whole team, opened the way clear for their runner and blocked the Yale players so that all their runner had to do was run. See? It was the team, not the runner, that did it.

The papers, the crowds, like and praise the individual players, but football is great because it is the teams, not the individuals, who play it when it is well played. Each individual player has to be good, skillful, perfect, but perfect only as the part of a perfect machine, which is the ideal.

William Thackeray and his daughter Anne

William Thackeray was among England's widely read Victorian novelists. His most popular work, *Vanity Fair,* created a long-lasting rivalry between him and his contemporary Charles Dickens. Thackeray was plagued by poor health throughout his life, and when his wife, Mary, proved mentally unable to care for their two daughters, the children went to live with their grandmother in Paris.

In June 1850 Thackeray was in London, absorbed in completing his novel *Pendennis*. He penned this letter to his daughter Anne upon her tenth birthday:

I am so busy with my work and so tired of writing that I can only write you a line or two. I'm delighted that you are so happy and that you can enjoy yourself, and that your friends are so kind to you. The way to have friends is to like people yourself, you see: and I hope you will have and keep aplenty.

I have been at home three days: think of that, not going out until at least near 8 o'clock to dinner. So my work is pretty well advanced and will be done by Sunday evening, I trust. Then comes printing and proof-correcting, and so forth, and by Thursday, I hope to see you young folk again and bring you back.

Don't make doggerel verses and spell badly for fun. There should be a lurking prettiness even in all buffoonery, and it requires an art which you don't know yet to make: good bad verse. To make bad ones is dull work.

And don't scribble faces at the bottom of your letters to ladies; they shouldn't be done unless they are clever.... I like you to make jokes to me because I can afford to tell you whether they are bad or good, or to scold you as now. But Mrs. Brookfield is too kind to do so, and when you write to her or to any other lady, you should write your very best. I don't mean be affected and use fine words, but be careful, grateful, and ladylike.

I did not dine until 9 o'clock last night and went to the opera afterwards, but the ballet bored me and I came away pretty soon. I think that's all I know. [In a few days], I will come down and let's take a small trip to the Isle of Wight or somewhere.

William Wilberforce and his son Samuel

William Wilberforce was an English parliamentary leader in the abolition of the slave trade. He exchanged more than six hundred letters with his third son, Samuel, starting when the lad was nine and the father was fifty-five; most focused on the lad's need for greater character improvement. Some boys would have rebelled against such intense paternal dominance, but Samuel became bishop of Oxford and of Winchester.

In September 1814 William Wilberforce sent this rather stern letter:

I was shocked to hear that you are nine years old. I thought it was eight. You must take great pains to prove to me that you are nine not in years only, but in head and heart and mind. Above all, my dearest Samuel, I am anxious to see decisive marks of your having to undergo *the great change*. . . .

A few weeks after Samuel's fourteenth birthday, his father remarked, "My dear boy, it is a great pleasure to me that you wish to know your faults."

Queen Victoria and Prince Albert and their son Albert Edward

Albert Edward ("Bertie"), who became King Edward VII of Great Britain and Ireland in 1902, was the eldest son of Queen Victoria and Prince Albert. Almost immediately after his birth, he was made Prince of Wales, and as a youth, traveled widely on the continent and visited the United States, Canada, and the Middle East. During his mother's long reign, he often represented the Crown at public functions and was known as a liberal patron of the arts and a leader of fashionable society. Bertie's love affairs and extravagent living, though, often offended the Queen. As king, he took a deep interest in foreign policy, and his travels helped to promote better international understanding, especially between France and England.

All those events lay in the future, however, when Bertie in November 1858 received this parental advice upon attaining his eighteenth birthday:

> Life is composed of duties, and in the due, punctual and cheerful performance of them the true Christian, true soldier and true gentleman is recognized.
>
> You will in future have rooms allotted to your sole use in order to give you an opportunity of learning how to occupy yourself unaided by others and to utilize your time in the best manner; that is, such time as may not be otherwise occupied by lessons, by the different tasks which will be given you by your director of studies, or reserved for exercise and recreation.
>
> A new sphere of life will open for you, in which you will have to be taught what to do and what not to do, a subject requiring study more important than any in which you have hitherto been engaged. For it is a subject of study and the most difficult one of your life: how to become a good man and a thorough gentleman. . . .
>
> Your personal allowance will be increased; but it is expected that you will carefully order your expenditure so as to remain strictly within the bounds of the sum allowed to you, which will be amply sufficient for your general requirements. . . .

You will try to emancipate yourself as much as possible from the thralldom of abject dependence for your daily wants of life on your servants. The more you can do for yourself, the greater will be your independence and real comfort.

Using Time Wisely

———

Arthur Schlesinger Jr.

Arthur Schlesinger Jr. ranks among America's leading historians today. His career spans more than a half century, marked by Pulitzer Prize awards for *The Age of Jackson* in 1946 and *A Thousand Days: J.F.K. in the White House,* published in 1966. After teaching at Harvard, he gained national attention as a special assistant to presidents John F. Kennedy and Lyndon B. Johnson. Today Schlesinger is the Albert Schweitzer Professor in Humanities at the City University of New York and appears frequently on television to provide a historical viewpoint on the news.

In an interview published in *The Ageless Spirit*, edited by Philip Berman and Connie Goldman, Schlesinger observed:

> In our seventies, time becomes the most precious of commodities. The thing I resent most is wasting it. Up until [your

seventieth birthday], time seemed infinite, but time is now finite. Every once in a while, when you go to a boring meeting or dinner party, you wonder what in the hell you are doing wasting your time. I try and repent and swear not to get myself in that kind of situation again. Certain things I just don't do anymore. For example, I never go to lectures unless I'm giving them myself. A number of things you cut off.

Vowing to Fight for Social Justice

Susan B. Anthony and her mother, Lucy Read Anthony

Susan B. Anthony is honored today as among America's most important feminist advocates. As a pioneering crusader for women's rights and president of the National American Woman Suffrage Movement, Anthony's work helped pave the way for the Nineteenth Amendment to the U.S. Constitution in 1920.

Born in 1820, she grew up in a moralistic home dominated by her Quaker father's zealous abolitionism. A precocious child, Anthony learned to read and write at the age of three. After attending several schools in upstate New York and then Philadelphia, Anthony became a school teacher near her family home in the Rochester area. Founding the Woman's State Temperance Society of New York, Anthony soon turned her attention to women's rights, and beginning in the 1850s, worked alongside her friends Elizabeth Cady Stanton and Amelia Bloomer. Anthony was also prominent in abolitionist efforts prior to the Civil War, and for more than fifty years until her death in 1906, her name was associated with political activism and courage.

On Susan B. Anthony's fiftieth birthday, in February 1870, she shared these sentiments with her mother:

It really seems tonight as if I were parting with something dear: saying goodbye to somebody I loved. In the last few hours, I have lived over nearly all of life's struggles, and the most painful is the memory of my mother's long and weary efforts to get her six children up into womanhood and manhood.

My constantly recurring thought and prayer now are that the coming fraction of the century, whether it be small or large, may witness nothing less worthy in my life than has the half just closed—that no word or act of mine may lessen its weight in the scale of truth and right.

Vowing to Live Outrageously

⚘

Maggie Kuhn

Maggie Kuhn was a social activist best known for her efforts on behalf of older Americans. When she and her five friends faced mandatory retirement at the age of sixty-five, they organized in 1971 the Consultation of Older and Younger Adults for Social Change, later renamed the "Grey Panthers." The 1978 World Almanac named her one of the twenty-five most influential women in America, and the *Ladies' Home Journal* honored her as one of America's one hundred most important women. Despite such accolades, she remained active, hardworking, and ever feisty. Among her aphorisms: "Old people constitute America's biggest untapped and undervalued human resource."

In an interview published in *The Ageless Spirit*, edited by Philip Berman and Connie Goldman, Kuhn affirmed at the age of eighty-six:

We oldsters have a lot to share. . . . I believe that there has to be a purpose and a goal to life. The secret of thriving and surviving is having a goal. [It] is absolutely essential, because it gives you the energy and the drive to do what you must do, and to get up when you feel like staying in bed.

I have plenty of goals! On my eightieth birthday, in fact, I vowed to myself that I would do something outrageous at least once a week, and for the past few years, I've been able to live up to that promise. On a more practical note, I've got daily chores to do. I have to get up early to feed the cats. And I like to take a morning bubble bath. I like to soak in the tub—right up to my neck, you know—just soak—and do a little exercising in the tub.

Then I'm ready to start my day. I like to eat breakfast and look at the paper and play with the cats and think about what's ahead for the day and do some immediate planning. And every day, every day is some surprise. I look for that. What's going to be new, what's new today? There is seldom a day without some element of surprise. I think in a sense surprise is synonymous with hope.

Permissions

Poem by Otto Frank in section entitled "Motivating One's Daughter" reprinted by permission of Doubleday, a division of Random House, from *The Diary of Anne Frank: The Critical Edition*, copyright 1996 by Anne Frank-Fonds.

"If We Didn't Have Birthdays" reprinted by permission of Alfred A. Knopf, a division of Random House, from *Happy Birthday to You!* by Dr. Seuss, TM and copyright 1959 and renewed 1987 by Dr. Seuss Enterprises, L.P.

"Twenty-four Years" reprinted by permission of New Directions Publishing Corporation, from *The Poems of Dylan Thomas*, copyright 1945 by the Trustees for the Copyrights of Dylan Thomas.

Poems by Albert Einstein and Samuel Gronnemann in selection entitled "Revealing Playfulness to a Friend" reprinted by permission of Princeton University Press, from *Albert Einstein: The Human Side*, copyright 1979 The Estate of Albert Einstein.

"Vacillation" reprinted by permission of Scribner, a division of Simon & Schuster, Inc., from *The Collected Works of W. B. Yeats, Volume 1: The Poems, Revised*, Richard J. Finneran, editor. Copyright 1933 by Macmillan Publishing Company and renewed 1961 by Bertha Georgia Yeats.

References

Adler, Bill. *Kids' Letters to President Kennedy.* New York: Morrow, 1961.

Asimov, Isaac. *In Memory Yet Green, The Autobiography of Isaac Asimov, 1920–1954.* New York: Avon, 1979.

Barrie, J. M. *Letters of J. M. Barrie.* Ed. Viola Meynell. London: Peter Davies, 1943.

Barry, Dave. *Dave Barry Turns 50.* New York: Crown, 1998.

Bedell, Madelon. *The Alcotts: Biography of a Family.* New York: Clarkson N. Potter, 1980.

Biracree, Tom. *Grandma Moses.* New York: Chelsea House, 1989.

Bredsdorff, Elias. *Hans Christian Andersen: The Story of His Life and Work, 1805–1875.* New York: Scribner, 1975.

Brooke, Rupert. *The Letters of Rupert Brooke.* Ed. Geoffrey Keynes. New York: Harcourt, Brace & World, 1968.

Browning, Robert, and Elizabeth Barrett Browning. *The Letters of Robert Browning and Elizabeth Barrett Browning, 1845–1846.* Ed. Elvin Kinter. Cambridge, Mass.: Harvard University Press, 1969.

Buber, Martin. *A Believing Humanism: My Testament, 1902–1965.* Translated by Maurice Friedman. New York: Simon & Schuster, 1967.

Cargas, Harry James, ed. *Telling the Tale: A Tribute to Elie Wiesel on the Occasion of his Sixty-fifth Birthday.* St. Louis: Time Being Books, 1993.

Chamberlain, James D., ed. *The Romance of Greeting Cards*. Cambridge: University Press of Cambridge, 1956.

Cohen, Morton N., ed. *The Selected Letters of Lewis Carroll*. London: Macmillan, 1982.

Creamer, Robert W. *Babe: The Legend Comes to Life*. New York: Simon & Schuster, 1974.

Cuomo, Mario. *Diaries of Mario Cuomo: The Campaign for Governor*. New York: Random House, 1984.

Dukas, Helen, and Hoffmann, Banesh. *Albert Einstein: The Human Side*. Princeton: Princeton University Press, 1979.

Eisenhower, Dwight D. *Letters to Mamie*. Ed. John S. D. Eisenhower. Garden City, N.Y.: Doubleday, 1978.

Eliot, T. S. *The Letters of T. S. Eliot*. Vol. 1. *1898–1922*. Ed. Valerie Eliot. New York: Harcourt, Brace, Jovanovich, 1988.

Emerson, Lidian Jackson. *The Selected Letters of Lidian Jackson Emerson*. Edited by Delores Bird Carpenter. Columbia, Mo.: University of Missouri Press, 1987.

Emerson, Ralph Waldo. *The Journals and Miscellaneous Notebooks of Ralph Waldo Emerson,* Vol. 7. *1838–1842*. Ed. A. W. Plumstead and Harrison Hayford. Cambridge, Mass.: Harvard University Press, 1969.

Flaubert, Gustave. *The Selected Letters of Gustave Flaubert*. Trans., ed. Francis Steegmuller. Freeport, N.Y.: Books for Libraries Press, 1971.

Frank, Anne. *The Diary of Anne Frank, The Critical Edition*. Ed. David Barnouw and Gerrold van der Stroom. Trans. Arnold J. Pomerans and B. M. Mooyaart-Doubleday. New York: Bantam Doubleday Dell, 1989.

Freeman, Martha, ed. *The Letters of Rachel Carson and Dorothy Freeman, 1952–1964.* Boston: Beacon, 1995.

Freud, Sigmund. *New Introductory Lectures on Psycho-Analysis and Other Works.* Trans. by James Strachey. London: Hogarth Press, 1964.

———. *The Complete Letters of Sigmund Freud to Wilhelm Fleiss, 1887–1904.* Trans., ed. Jeffrey Moussaieff Masson. Cambridge, Mass.: Harvard University Press, 1985.

——— and Zweig, Arnold. *The Letters of Sigmund Freud and Arnold Zweig.* Ed. Ernest L. Freud. Trans. Elaine and William Robson-Scott. New York: Harcourt, Brace & World, 1970.

Frost, Robert. *The Letters of Robert Frost to Louis Untermeyer.* New York: Holt, Rinehart & Winston, 1963.

Fulford, Roger, ed. *Your Dear Letter, Private Correspondence of Queen Victoria and the Crown Princess of Prussia, 1865–1871.* New York: Scribner's, 1971.

Fuller, Margaret. *The Letters of Margaret Fuller.* Vol. 3. *1842–1844.* Ed. Robert N. Hudspeth. Ithaca, N.Y.: Cornell University Press, 1984.

Gibran, Kahlil. *The Kahil Gibran Reader.* Seacaucus, N.J.: Carol Publishing, 1995.

——— and Mary Haskell. *Beloved Prophet: The Love Letters of Kahlil Gibran and Mary Haskell.* Ed. Virginia Hsilu. New York: Knopf, 1972.

Goldstein, Bobbye S., ed. *Birthday Rhymes, Special Times.* New York: Bantam Doubleday Dell, 1993.

Gottfried, Martin. *George Burns and the Hundred-Year Dash.* New York: Simon & Schuster, 1998.

Greene, Graham. *A Sort of Life*. New York: Simon & Schuster, 1971.

Haggard, H. Rider. *The Private Diaries of Sir H. Rider Haggard, 1914–1925*. Ed. D. S. Higgins. New York: Stein & Day, 1980.

Hallam, Arthur Henry. *The Letters of Arthur Henry Hallam*. Ed. Jack Kolb. Columbus: Ohio University Press, 1981.

Hemingway, Ernest. *Selected Letters, 1917–1961*. Ed. Carlos Baker. New York: Scribner, 1981.

Hoffman, Edward. *The Right to Be Human: A Biography of Abraham Maslow*. Rev. ed. New York: McGraw-Hill, 1999.

————. *The Book of Fathers' Wisdom: Paternal Advice From Moses to Bob Dylan*. Secaucus, N.J.: Carol Publishing, 1997.

Hoffman, Laurel B. *The Book of Mothers' Wisdom: Maternal Advice from the Queen of Sheba to Princess Di*. Secaucus, N.J.: Carol Publishing, 1998.

Hopkins, Gerard Manley. *The Poems of Gerard Manley Hopkins*. 4th ed. Ed. W. H. Gardner and N. H. Mackenzie. London: Oxford University Press, 1967.

Janeczko, Paul B., ed. *Strings: A Gathering of Family Poems*. Scarsdale, N.Y.: Bradbury Press, 1984.

Jong, Erica. *Fear of Fifty, A Midlife Memoir*. New York: HarperCollins, 1994.

Larkin, Philip. *Selected Letters of Philip Larkin, 1940–1985*. Ed. Anthony Thwaite. New York: Farrar, Straus & Giroux, 1992.

Lash, Joseph P. *Love, Eleanor: Eleanor Roosevelt and Her Friends*. Garden City, N.Y.: Doubleday, 1982.

L'Engle, Madeleine. *A Circle of Quiet*. New York: Farrar, Straus & Giroux, 1972.

Levy, Jacques. *Cesar Chavez: Autobiography of La Causa*. New York: Norton, 1975.

Lewis, C. S. *Letters to Children*. Ed. Lyle W. Dorsett and Marjorie Lamp Mead. New York: Macmillan, 1965.

Marchand, Leslie A., ed. *Bryon's Letters and Journals*. Cambridge, Mass.: Harvard University Press, 1975.

Murry, John Middleton. *The Letters of John Middleton Murry to Katherine Mansfield*. Ed. C.A. Hankin. London: Constable, 1983.

Marx, Arthur. *My Life With Groucho: A Son's Eye View*. London: Robson Books, 1988.

———. *The Secret Life of Bob Hope*. New York: Barricade Books, 1993.

Marx, Harpo. *Harpo Speaks!* New York: Limelight Editions, 1961.

Mencken, H. L. *The Diary of H. L. Mencken*. Ed. Charles A. Fecher. New York: Knopf, 1989.

Milne, A. A. *Autobiography*. New York: Dutton, 1939.

Morgan, Ted. *FDR, a Biography*. New York: Simon & Schuster, 1985.

Nash, Ogden. *Selected Poetry of Ogden Nash*. New York: Little, Brown, 1995.

Potter, Beatrix. *The Journal of Beatrix Potter, From 1881 to 1897*. Transcribed from her code writing by Leslie Linder. London: Warne, 1966.

Ritchie, Hester Thackeray, ed. *Thackeray and His Daughter*. New York: Harper & Brothers, 1924.

Roosevelt, Theodore. *The Letters of Theodore Roosevelt*. Ed. Elting E. Morison. Cambridge, Mass.: Harvard University Press, 1951.

Russell, Phillips. *Emerson, the Wisest American*. New York: Brentano's, 1929.

Spoto, Donald. *Marilyn Monroe, the Biography*. New York: HarperCollins, 1993.

Steinbeck, John. *A Life in Letters*. Eds. Elaine Steinbeck and Robert Wallsten. New York: Viking, 1975.

Thomas, Dylan. *Letters to Vernon Watkins*. Ed. Vernon Watkins. New York: New Directions, 1957.

Tillich, Paul. *My Travel Diary: 1936*. Ed. Jerald C. Brauer, trans. Maria Pelikan. New York: Harper & Row, 1970.

Tolkien, J. R. R. *The Letters of J. R. R. Tolkien*. Ed. Humphrey Carpenter. Boston: Houghton Mifflin, 1981.

Trillin, Calvin. *Too Soon to Tell*. New York: Farrar, Straus & Giroux, 1995.

Truman, Harry. *Dear Bess, the Letters From Harry to Bess Truman, 1910–1959*. Ed. Robert H. Ferrell. New York: Norton, 1983.

Truman, Margaret. *Letters From Father*. New York: Arbor House, 1981.

Twain, Mark. *Mark Twain's Letters*. Vol. 1. Ed. Albert Bigelow Paine. New York: Harper & Brothers, 1917.

Valentine, Alan. *Fathers to Sons, Advice Without Consent*. Norman: University of Oklahoma Press, 1963.

Victoria, Queen of Great Britain. *Further Letters of Queen Victoria*. Translated from the German by J. Pudney and Lord Sudley and edited by Hector Polito. London: Thornton Butterworth, 1938.

Walker, Marianne. *Margaret Mitchell and John Marsh, The Love Story Behind Gone With the Wind*. Atlanta: Peachtree Publishers, 1993.

Weintraub, Stanley. *Victoria, an Intimate Biography*. New York: Dutton, 1987.

White, Anna MacBride, and Jeffares, A. Norman, eds. *Gonne-Yeats Letters, 1893–1938*. New York: Norton, 1992. St. Louis: Time Being Books, 1993.

White, E. B. *Letters of E. B. White*. Ed. Dorothy Lobrano Guth. New York: Harper & Row, 1976.

Whitman, Walt. *Selected Letters of Walt Whitman*. Ed. Edwin Haviland. Iowa City: University of Iowa Press, 1990.

Woolf, Virginia. *A Moment's Liberty: The Shorter Diary*. Ed. Anne Oliver Bell. New York: Harcourt Brace Jovanovich, 1982.

Wordsworth, Dorothy. *Journals of Dorothy Wordsworth*. Vol. 1. Ed. E. de Selincourt. London: Macmillan, 1952.

Yeats, William B. *The Collected Poems of W. B. Yeats*. New York: Macmillan, 1962.